More Than Enough

Discover Your Limitless Potential and Live Your Bravest Dream

LARA HABIG

Disclaimer: This book is not intended as a substitute for the medical advice of physicians. The reader should regularly consult a physician in matters relating to his/her health and particularly with respect to any symptoms that may require diagnosis or medical attention. Although the author and publisher have made every effort to ensure that the information in this book was correct at press time, the author and publisher do not assume and hereby disclaim any liability to any party for any loss, damage, or disruption caused by errors or omissions, whether such errors or omissions result from negligence, accident, or any other cause. In order to maintain their anonymity in some instances, the author has changed some of the names of individuals and places, and may have changed some identifying characteristics and details such as physical properties, occupations and places of residence.

ISBN: 978-1-943784-06-6
LCCN: 2015916977

Printed in the United States of America

DEDICATION

I would like to dedicate this book to my sons, Daniel and Tyler. Without your love, encouragement, and support this book would have never been written. Thank you for making me smile even on the darkest days. Love you both very much!

RAVING REVIEWS

"Thoughtfully Written For Our Busy World!"

"I found this to be an easy read... *thoughtfully* written for our busy world and *purely* shared as the truths of your precious heart. You are so loved and admired. Your story will help shape stronger lives... even SAVE lives. Your authentic life will continue to bless others abundantly. God is using you daily in a mighty and deep way. I was blessed immensely from your spirit-led book with God's seal of approval! Many things you shared resonated with me and I am applying your noted healing and growing methods."

— Stacy Paetz

"Generous Steps Are Easy To Follow!"

"Your loving and generous steps are easy to follow, and will be helpful to those seeking a path to find inner peace through self-love, on their journey to realizing that they too... are ENOUGH."

— Glenda Meyer

"Identified With Every Piece Of This Book!"

"Thank you for writing this book. And just Thank GOD for you. I laughed, I cried, I identified with every piece of this book and it touched my soul. If I could have written a book (I always wanted to) - this is what I would have written. So again, THANK YOU! I'm always relieved to know there is someone else going through the same things and even more so when it is things that are so very similar. I'm also relieved to know that I am handling situations 'properly' or attempting to go down the right path. But I also know that I still have work to do. We have many obstacles to overcome. This book has given me a spark again to keep moving forward towards knowing that I/we are enough where we are at this point in time."

−Jennie Boller

"A Must Read For Anyone Seeking More Satisfaction!"

"*More Than Enough* is a must read for anyone seeking more satisfaction and peace in their everyday life! Lara's profound spiritual journey and real world stories will make you cry and then make your heart soar. I found myself nodding in agreement as she described parts of her life before Limitless Soul. With the steps she outlines in each easily digestible chapter, you will be well on your way to loving yourself, and discovering your soul's purpose. I enjoyed every minute of this relatable read and I can't wait for the next one!"

−Lacey Ring-Verbik, Imagine Virtual Assistant Service

"A Necessity For Health, Happiness And Fulfillment!"

"As I read *More Than Enough*, I was struck by how many of the daily destroyers of 'self love' applied to my own life... and how I perceived my value. I have been known to apologize profusely and assume responsibility for things that weren't my fault, because as Lara states in the book, 'I was merciless with myself.' Additionally, I would put my needs last, because I didn't want to let down anyone who requested my assistance. After all, there would be time for me to engage in personal resilience later, right? *More Than Enough* is a 'must read' and important in understanding that 'self love' is not a luxury... but, a necessity for health, happiness and fulfillment!"

– *Mary Burkhart*

"Thoughtfully Laid Out And Easy To Understand!"

"It is very clear that Lara is someone who practices what she teaches in *More Than Enough*. The book is thoughtfully laid out and easy to understand. If for some strange reason I could only choose one chapter from this book to share with everyone, my pick would be Chapter 3 because there is nothing better, in my opinion, than experiencing 'being fully present, here and now.' Thank you Lara for the privilege of reading your work before its release, it was a true pleasure!"

– *Shelly Allen, Master Empowerment Coach, ShellyAllen.com*

"This Book Resonated With Me!"

"Many principles of this book resonated with me - self love, the importance of nutrition and exercise, recognizing and committing to priorities, setting boundaries, asking for help, meditation and time in nature, etc. Given my finance background, it probably comes as no surprise that I strongly agree with the importance of being aware of your financial situation. Making responsible, sound decisions you can feel good about, not just in the moment, but also long-term plays an enormous role in both mental and physical health."

—*Amber Winchester, Finance Professional, Retired at 38*

"Renewal Of Self Acceptance For Me!"

"I started your book and could not put it down. Awesome work. Good methods and personal examples. Loved the chapter setup with summaries. I walked on air for several days and can still evoke that feeling by thinking of your book. I needed to renew myself and your book was right on time. I'm blessed to read it before it was printed. So exhilarating! Renewal of self acceptance for me. Bless you for sharing. Perfect chapter summaries to lead the way to *enough*."

—*Rita J. Rose*

"I Accepted Your Challenge!"

"I, too, did not think I was GOOD ENOUGH most of my life. I accepted your challenge about walking 15 minutes, outside, everyday. At first, I didn't think it would make that much of a difference. Boy was I wrong! Your book has made me realize that I need to set boundaries in my life and that it's okay to say NO to people. My girls are grown with their own families. It's time for me! It's time to live my life for me!"

—*Cindy Wood*

"I Realize How Important It Is To Take Care Of Myself!"

"I now realize how important it is for me to take care of myself. I neglect myself when it comes to eating right and exercising. I need to be 'quiet', my busy brain can take over which greatly diminishes my quality of rest/sleep. It is okay and essential to take care of myself! Eat, sleep, exercise for a new me!"

—Julie Meyer

"You Made Me Feel Like It Was Okay To Slow Down!"

"You've got a gentle way of saying what so many of us need to hear. As a type-A personality, I'm used to pushing and pushing and when I was finished with the book, you made me feel like it was okay to slow down and focus on myself, something that society in general doesn't value. After all, we're 'human beings, not human-doings.' LOVED that line. Overall, the book is comforting because you open up and tell your story. I love hearing stories from fellow human beings, usually because we can all relate to one-another that way. Thank you for telling yours."

—Jay Hankins

"An Interesting And Compelling Read!"

"I really enjoyed and appreciate the opportunity to read your manuscript! It was definitely an interesting and compelling read, especially because it was backed by your personal experiences. Your book reminds me a lot of one of my favorites, *How to Win Friends and Influence People* by Dale Carnegie."

—Ryan Van Slyke

"I Started Reading And Could Not Stop!"

"I started reading and could not stop. *More Than Enough* allows the reader to connect with the author and clients in the book. This book allows the reader to be guided on how to feel ENOUGH without being judgmental or all-knowing. Clearly written by someone who truly knows how hard it is to move from the past to the present. Wow. A must for my library. I will be referring to ENOUGH regularly as I continue on my journey of learning to know I am ENOUGH."

— Kenda Hamersley, Mom, Grandmother, and Teacher

"A Perfect Blend Of Self Help Ideas!"

"*More Than Enough* is a perfect blend of self help ideas and interesting autobiography. Although it is best read slowly to focus on each self care suggestion, the book in its entirety is a very pleasant, easy read. Ideas and suggestions abound in an encouraging, supportive commentary. This is a great go-to book for personal growth and positive affirmation. Best of all, it offers inspiration!"

— Lorie Dilanchian (Choir Director, Danville Community Schools, Danville, Indiana)

"I Love The Useful, Practical Advice!"

"I love the useful, practical advice. Lara does not take a 'one size fits all' approach. She celebrates that individuals have to use the approach that works best in their life. She skillfully combines that with specific suggestions anyone can use."

— Lisa Dumeyer

"Motivates Me To Care More For Myself Without Guilt!

"Lara shared insight regarding the same worries I've kept in the back of my mind for years. Things I've struggled to release. Her positive reminders and support motivates me to care more for myself and love myself...without guilt. Very much appreciate the 'sparks' and compassion this angel has for those in need."

— *Wendy Crandall*

"Simple And Profound Life Changing Practices!"

"I found Lara's book to be inspiring because it is so real! It's an amazing treasure of seemingly simple but profound and life changing practices that she used to heal herself from the 'I am not enough' syndrome that is so pervasive in our culture. She speaks from her heart and her experience, offering advice we can trust. For me, reading Lara's book was like listening to a dear friend, sharing her wisdom from 'the trenches' of life and showing practical steps to reclaim our self-love as our birthright."

— *Elizabeth Haines, Client Attraction Magic for Healers, Therapists, and Coaches at ehaines.com*

"Great Motivational Book For All Aspects Of Your Life!"

"Great motivational book for all aspects of your life. In just 3 days it has changed my perspective and made me question what is really important, what can I say no to and how can I take better care of myself. I have already stepped out of my box and feel energized and relaxed."

— *LaDonna Sloan*

"I Enjoyed Learning Different Ways To Deal With Stress!"

"I enjoyed reading *More Than Enough* and learning of different ways to deal with stress. I do take advantage of the silence of nature often in my own backyard. At church the Pastor speaks of evil trying to talk you down in your head and I loved the way you describe it as 'mind chatter'. It is important not to listen to it when the chatter is negative."

– Vicki Jo Lee

"The Truths Are Real And Alive Inside Every One Of Us!"

"Lara reaches deep inside herself and pulls out the truths the vast majority of people don't like to even think about. The truths are real and alive inside every one of us, and her step-by-step advice can surely lead anyone down a path to recovery from their problems."

– Tyler Habig

"I Agree Whole-Heartedly With Lara's Advice!"

"I agree whole-heartedly with Lara's advice when it comes to taking care of ourselves. All too often, we tend to 'outdo' ourselves by over-scheduling our day. I can attest to this because I tend to be 'doing' all the time and forget to schedule time for just ME. I need to consciously force myself to get outside to walk and enjoy nature, while just taking in the moment. I'm going to start setting aside daily time where I can just BE!"

– Rose B., Elementary School Secretary

"I Really Enjoyed It!"

"Great job!! I really enjoyed it! Thank you for sharing your book with us. "

— *Valerie V.*

"Felt As If I Was On The Path Of Self-Healing!"

"The moment I began reading Lara Habig's words on clearing my mind of its chatter, and the Be Still concept, I immediately felt as if I was on the path of self-healing. Being shown how to see that I am *Enough* has given me the courage to take in her most important message, that it is not selfish to take care of myself. I eagerly await a follow up on this life changing topic of self love."

— *Lauren Beretta, Massage Therapist, Doula, and Energy Worker*

"A Book That Every Woman Must Read!"

"*More Than Enough* is a book that every woman must read, especially in today's society where it's acceptable and sometimes expected for women to play small. If you have ever experienced negative self-talk, indecisive self-doubt, or self-deprecating dialogue, then Lara Habig's powerful yet compassionate voice will certainly help you *Discover Your Limitless Potential and Live Your Bravest Dream.*"

-- *Lena Anani, Author of OMG Do It Now: Be the Voice You Want to Hear in the World*

CONTENTS

ACKNOWLEDGEMENTS

Dr. Barb Koewler: An understanding and loving friend who has supported me through the unbelievable ups and downs of my life. You remained a good friend even though I fought taking your health advice! For that, I thank you for letting me learn on my own and for not saying "I told you so!" I promise I will listen from now on! Love you!

Andrea Beaman: The short time we worked together was life-changing. Your focus on self-love altered the way I viewed my life. Thank you for blessing me with your gifts. You laid a foundation that cannot be shattered.

Carmina McGee: I am in awe of your extensive knowledge and how it applies to the healing of my body. You have reminded me often that I am in charge of my support team. Thank you for guiding me with love, information, and discernment to make the best decisions for my health and my body.

Lena Anani: My patient and caring book coach who believed in me even when I didn't believe in myself. Thank you for your support and your ability to flow with my crazy life as I was writing this book. You are much appreciated!

Melissa Harnish: You're a dear friend who has stuck with me through good times and bad. We have laughed and cried together, all the while knowing there would be brighter days ahead. Thank you for your non-judgmental and never ending support.

Sonia Barnes: Thank you for your consistent friendship even as my life took many twists and turns. You jumped on my roller coaster ride of a life and kept cheering me on. You are much appreciated and loved! Thank you for being YOU!

Rose Berg: We have spent many days together since first meeting when our children were preschool age. Memories I will cherish forever. Each moment has been peppered with laughter and tears, sometimes fear, but always love. Thank you for being YOU!

To the AUMC Ladies: (Carol, LaDonna, Valerie, Lisa, Penny, Pamela, Vicki, Melissa, Rose, Sonia and Miss Betty) Thank you for your friendship, guidance, and love over the years. You each have a place in my heart that laid the foundation for who I am today.

Dr. Shaun Dumas: You were a Godsend as I struggled to get well last winter. I looked forward to every acupuncture treatment because you gave me hope for wellness. Thank you for being you!

And, of course, to my family: I know you all don't necessarily understand my journey, but you have loved and supported me nonetheless.

Mom and Dad: (Layden and Suzie) Thank you for reminding me to stand up for myself and live my own bravest dream.

Steven: I know you thought you were going to be the villain in this book, but really, I am thankful you were as hard on me as you were. Through that experience, I am stronger and better able to handle the world as it is. Much love and thanks to you.

Brian: To the brother who is *perfect* in every way, or at least so he reminds me! Thank you for your support and love. You make me smile as I know you always have my back.

Lisa: To my little sister who was spoiled and got everything she wanted! Just kidding, you are amazing, loving, and supportive. Without you and your sweet girls (Kylie and Kaci), there would have been many more sad days. You picked me up when I was down and reminded me to keep going when things got tough. Thank you for being there for me no matter what. You have taught me, by example, true self-love.

Liana Chaouli: Thank you to my mentor at ImageTherapists.com who continued to hold the vision for this book and the work that I do in the world when I couldn't see it myself. She gets up under you "like a boulder" to support and push you to your God-given destination of only the very highest and best. Much heartfelt gratitude to you and your team for not letting me stay small and hide!

And, of course, to all my beautiful friends, family, and mentors I didn't mention above: Every one of you has played an important part in my life and in the writing of this book. I am forever grateful and honored to be a part of your life–whether it was for a short time or a lifetime. Thank you for loving and supporting me even when I couldn't do it for myself.

HOW TO READ THIS BOOK

There are several ways you can read this book. Of course, it can be read straight through, beginning with the *Introduction*. The *Introduction* is a must-read to fully discern the rest of the book. Another option is to read the *Introduction* and pick ANY chapter that interests you. Read that specific chapter repeatedly for a month, working through the questions and challenges I offer. Take your time as you work through each chapter, recording your notes in the back of the book. Read this book as you are led, in order or broken into segments. Regardless of *how* you read it, embrace this book as your guide to a luxurious life of self-love and deep satisfaction!

INTRODUCTION

*"Low self-esteem is like driving through life
with the hand-brake on."* – Maxwell Maltz

For many years now I have felt like something deep inside of me was screaming to be heard. On most days, I ignored it. It was easy to dismiss my soul's calling, or so I thought. When my crisis of faith intersected with health issues and a divorce after twenty-five years of marriage, listening to my soul's calling became my guiding light on the dark days. That light was my soul, or God spark as I refer to it, crying to be heard.

When I finally began to *hear* what my soul was trying to tell me, I realized that my past pain and suffering were not in vain. It was a conduit to my soul's calling here on earth. It was guiding me all along to do what I came here to do in this time and place.

What if that is the case with you as well?

What if your pain is your access point to your purpose?

What if your suffering is the conduit to *Your Soul's Calling*?

For me, this journey has led me down a road of helping others who believe they are not enough. Depression, anxiety, eating disorders, self-hate, and self-neglect may be ruling your life, like it did mine. Questions run through most of our minds, like: Are you thin enough yet? Smart enough? Tall? Pretty? Enough money in your bank account? Are you *enough* to pursue your dream?

Am I enough? That is what most every person wants to know at their core.

What is it going to take for you to believe you are enough?

Sooner or later it seems we all entertain the idea that we aren't enough. The problem isn't that it only happens once or even twice. It can be so ingrained in our psyche that our self-esteem is annihilated. Like a cancer, it can spread quickly and dangerously.

Afflicting most everyone in the world at one time or another, a negative self-image affects our energy and our spirit. Quickly, it can conquer every area of our lives. It can take down a person's whole world. Entire families and generations. We crave something and look everywhere for it. We become desperate, seeking fulfillment in other people, food, drugs, work, anything and everything, attempting to dull the pain of not enough and never succeeding.

Maybe you're going through a divorce or maybe you detest yourself. Been there, done that. Sometimes not believing you're enough comes out as anger, depression, lack of self-care, fear, feeling worthless, or even people-pleasing. I know exactly how you feel, and lived through it to tell the tales. Those days when you loathe yourself so much that you can't get out of bed. Those days when you cry yourself to sleep or can't look at yourself in the mirror.

Self-esteem is a confidence and satisfaction in yourself. It's also tied to your own self-respect. It's how you think and feel about yourself. It can affect every area of your life, leaving no stone unturned. Your health, relationships, even your job may be affected by the way you value (or don't value) yourself. It can help you hold your head high and feel proud of yourself and what you do, even when things don't seem to be going well. Self-esteem gives you the courage to try new things and the power to believe in yourself. It's a measure of how you see yourself and how you feel about your life.

I do want to make it clear that having self-esteem isn't about bragging! A healthy self-esteem is an inner knowledge that you are worthy exactly as you are. You accept and love yourself in this moment—flaws and all!

If self-esteem is a measure of how you see yourself and how you feel about your life, it would make sense to have *good* self-esteem; we would need to do things for ourselves and our lives that honor the amazing creations that we each are. Essentially, to have a healthy self-esteem, loving ourselves is a must.

Not loving yourself is like watching dominos fall. One right after the other. Choosing to not eat healthy or exercise will send you down the road of challenging health issues. Choosing to allow anger to overcome you will most likely result in hurting others or, if pushed inward, depression and health issues.

Not loving yourself can also present itself in one or more of these ways:

- You get frustrated easily.
- You have an eating disorder.
- You may socially withdraw.
- You have an inability to see yourself *squarely* or to be fair to yourself.
- You can't accept compliments.
- You neglect yourself.
- You treat yourself badly, but not other people.
- You are reluctant to take on challenges.
- You are reluctant to put yourself first.
- You are reluctant to trust your own opinion.
- You expect little out of life for yourself.

Folks who struggle with self-love can't believe they are ENOUGH. No matter how hard they try or how often they hear it from others, they can't seem to believe they are good enough.

Self-love is a gentle acceptance, an unconditional sense of support and caring, and a core of compassion for yourself. It is an abiding willingness to meet your own needs, allow yourself to feel and think whatever you feel and think, and to see yourself as essentially worthy, good, valuable, and belonging in the world, deserving of happiness. And, most importantly, a belief that you are ENOUGH, as you are, in this moment. Self-love is developed early in life, and if childhood experiences damage our sense of self significantly, a lack of self-love can hurt us for a lifetime.

We need to have a healthy self-esteem and practice self-love because it affects every aspect of our lives. It's essential, because:

- Without it, we can crumble and not show up for our life.
- It helps us feel good about ourselves.
- It gives us courage to try new things.
- It helps us honor and respect ourselves, even when we make mistakes.
- It encourages us to make healthy decisions for our minds and bodies.

All this does not mean that a person with good self-esteem discounts others, but instead they value themselves and ensure their own feelings or needs are not discounted.

– My Story –

In the past, I thought it horribly selfish to say I loved myself. I didn't understand people around me that took time out of their day to care for themselves. True self-love isn't greedy, selfish or egoistical. Somewhere I learned it was selfish – almost sinful – to take care of yourself. I believed it was greedy to take time to work out or relax. Churches I attended in the past didn't help much either. Churches are set up to encourage us to volunteer. Coming from the background I did, I pushed myself by helping others until I was wiped out because that's what I thought I HAD to do.

When I finally got off the hamster wheel of taking care of everyone else but myself, I realized how important and honorable self-love really is. I see now that in order to have a loving relationship with others we must have a loving relationship with ourselves FIRST, and that means practicing self-love! The problem when we don't love ourselves or take care of ourselves is we will not feel good– physically or emotionally. And, when we don't feel good, we can't fully love those around us. We can even be resentful towards others who do honor themselves.

My reality not so long ago was difficulty, depression, anxiety, eating disorders, self-hate, and self-neglect. My low self-confidence would further fuel me into not showing up for ME. Un-kept commitments to myself led me into an even deeper depression. Spiritually and emotionally, I was unfulfilled. Empty.

My early years were filled with stress, unpredictability and sorrow. As a child, I didn't know how to have fun. I was the overly responsible sibling, always wanting to make sure everyone was happy and their needs were met. Not understanding why, I also carried this burden into adulthood. It was peace at all costs. Shame and fear were my constant companions, never allowing me to trust myself or my own feelings. Don't talk, don't trust and don't feel were the subconscious messages I would send myself. I tended toward impulsive decisions and couldn't fully share who I was out of fear.

When I was twenty one years old, I married my hometown boyfriend, who was six years older. He was very predictable and provided a feeling of safety. Both of us were raised in a Protestant, Christian church and cherished our traditional marriage. Prior to marrying, we agreed on having three or four children. After we had two wonderful boys, he wasn't interested in having additional children. However, I felt strongly in my heart that God was still calling us to have at least one more child. This heartbreak sent me into a deep depression. I began to feel so incomplete, I could barely function on some days.

For years, we tried counseling. However, we could never come to a mutual agreement or understanding. Counselors called what we were experiencing a *classic gridlock*. They told us we needed to become friends again and start over before we could even discuss the issues with love, empathy, and compassion. That never happened. I felt unheard, unseen and abandoned. My dream of having additional children solely rested on another human being's choice, and it was not to be.

During these difficult years, my health began to decline. Along with the depression, at thirty-nine I had a complete hysterectomy due to endometriosis. Needless to say, I was devastated. Although I was ever so thankful for our two boys I was able to birth, my dream of having additional children was not to happen.

A perceived lack of support in my life made it seem I had nowhere to turn. I was the woman on the sidelines watching life pass by. Strangely enough, from the outside, things were picture perfect... successful husband, successful home business, beautiful home, two amazing and talented sons, a great school system, fabulous vacations, a tight-knit community, and church family. EveryTHING the normal American family desires and more.

But, on the inside, I was dying. Utter despair and depression overtook me. Antidepressants became my safety net to stay in my hollow life. Attempting to dull the pain of not enough, but never succeeding, I knew it wasn't lady-like to be angry at others, so I subconsciously turned my anger inwards. After all, I was a *good* Christian woman and we loved everyone... everyone except myself. I was merciless with myself.

– Healing Self-Hatred –

Although many negative beliefs were implanted at an early age, as an adult, I believed the lies my own mind chatter pounded at me. Lies like: You are fat. You are ugly. You are stupid. God wasn't paying attention when he made you. You are not enough. You have to do more. Be more. You are a mistake. Lies and more lies. I believed them. I didn't know any different. I suspect the early sexual abuse and generations of alcohol addiction played into these beliefs.

In order to numb myself from the pain that antidepressants couldn't begin to alleviate, I made myself even busier. I taught Bible Studies, attended other Bible Studies, ran a moms' group, volunteered at the kids' schools, worked two part-time jobs including my own marketing company, volunteered at the church (Christian education, marketing committee, youth groups), and volunteered for the local education foundation and more. And, frankly, for years I appeared to be very successful at juggling all those balls.

My health continued a downward spiral with what seemed to be no return. Symptoms such as fatigue, anxiety, weight gain, hair loss, puffy face, sweating, difficulty sleeping, irritability, muscle weakness, depression, dry skin, and forgetfulness were beginning to worsen. I was struggling on many days to even get out of bed. I kept telling myself I was just in a funk and needed to get out more!

I made myself busier and busier. None of which seemed to take the pain away, though, of not enough.

I was surrounded by people and things but felt ever so isolated. Exhausted, I was hanging on by an invisible thread. Even with counseling, my marriage was also crumbling at a rapid rate.

Looking back, my entire life has been the ENOUGH message. Like many of us, I never thought I was enough or had enough. I thought that I had to do do do all the time. Although I felt strongly led by God to have more children, I believed that I HAD to have more children before I was complete. It was a horrible feeling to know your dreams were in someone else's hands and you didn't have any say. Struggling against my circumstances, I became very angry at God, my ex-husband and the world as I fought my inner demons of not being enough.

– The Spark Of Hope –

Although it seemed my life was imploding, there was always a small spark inside that kept me going. I knew deep in my soul that there was more to life than this box I had put myself in.

Due to my perplexing health issues, I became desperate for nutrition counseling and was led to a Godly spiritual leader for assistance. What began with nutrition information became a turning point towards a new life of deep satisfaction and complete fulfillment in all areas of my life. In many ways, I knew all along that I desired more of God and thought I could get *it* at a church. What I realized, though, was that God was inside of me the entire time and I just needed to learn how to listen and trust.

I would remind myself often that my soul was limitless and began to believe that anything was possible. Each day, I would release and reconnect to myself. Daily, I would do a reset to remind myself of the possibilities. Silencing that inner critic was my job 24/7. All the answers began with looking within. Answering the hard questions.

Gradually, each day built upon itself and with each step I became stronger. When the dark days began to diminish, I could see I was ENOUGH just as I was. An acceptance and love for myself emerged, and with it dormant healing abilities arose from the ashes of what was my life. Angels appeared and spoke to me. When others were needing healing, God would speak through me—usually in a language I didn't understand.

As scared as I was of this newfound treasure, I embraced the new me, allowing God and His angels to work in my life. Not surprisingly, confidence and passion for life returned with a vengeance, and my business Limitless Soul was born!

When I first began thinking about *loving myself*, I couldn't even say the words. I would cringe. I knew intuitively that I needed to practice self-love, but I still couldn't say the words. So, instead, I began the practices outlined in this book as a foundation for loving myself, until I could say the words. With each step, I gained confidence in myself and my place in the world. Slowly but surely, the dominos I had pushed over with my self-hatred gradually began standing back up on their own.

I learned how to do many of the things I talk about in the following chapters. These seemingly simple practices were the beginning of an entirely new outlook on life for me. I finally came to realize that I was enough just as I am. I no longer had to look outside of my life to know I'm okay. No one else can give you the desires of your heart. The perfect job, life, body, accomplishments, or amount of money in the bank will not EVER be able to tell you and sustain for you that you are enough. There's never enough if you need something outside of yourself. It's only what's going on in your own consciousness, your own soul, that can prevent you from being happy.

This book is for you if you are not sure if you're enough. It will help you realize your true value and encourage you into pursuing your own bravest dreams. It begins with loving yourself. There are many ways to practice self-love and this book will touch on the main practices I implemented in my life.

You can expect the same results I received when implementing these practices. Results such as:

- Release self-limiting beliefs that hold you back from greatness.

- Release old patterns and open yourself up to unlimited possibilities.
- Reconnect with your soul's desire to enjoy the beauty of life.
- Renew your divine commitment to self-care and self-worth.
- Renew your spiritual connection.
- Renew your commitment to pursuing your greatest dreams.
- You will value and love yourself.
- You will know you are ENOUGH.
- You will have HOPE.
- Become a healthier person — mind, body and spirit.
- You will learn how to hear from God.
- Fears will fade and confidence will soar right into your own bravest dream.

I am honored and humbled to offer my own journey as an example of realizing you are ENOUGH. Consider me your *spark of hope* tour guide! If you can believe in yourself with the little spark of hope that's left, you can soar into your own bravest dream. I can help you see your limitless potential even when you can't see it for yourself. But, most importantly, you will begin to see your past pain and suffering can be the conduit to your greatest gift to the world— *Your Soul's Calling.* Enjoy!

BE STILL

"Taking time to do nothing often brings everything into perspective." — Doe Zantamata

In today's fast-paced society the majority of us are on information overload: exhausted, worn out, and depleted. We are tired. Our bodies are screaming for healthy, nutritious food and eight hours of uninterrupted sleep. Our minds are ready to explode from all the information and advertising we take in every day.

We seem to be running around non-stop, sometimes not even sure where we are going! We fill our days with endless electronic communication (internet, TV, video games, cell phones, movies) and constant driving to/from activities, including meals on the run. Many of my days included picnics in the school parking lot while my boys ate a quick meal before their sport or band practice. We go go go. We do do do. We put out fires all day long. The urgent tasks seem to scream at us, while the important tasks silently stand nearby waiting patiently.

In our daily lives many of us even resort to *praying on the run*, hoping even a smidgen of what we request gets through the busy lines. We ask question after question. We ask for help and wonder why we don't get answers. There is so much noise in our lives we couldn't hear the answers anyway. Physically, spiritually, many of us are depleted.

That was me. As my body was running on empty, I was forced to *Be Still*.

I encourage you to try it before you are forced! *Be Still*. Just sit there. Stare out the window at nature as long as you possibly can! Notice how you feel. What does it feel like? How long can you sit still with nothing to do? Time moves slowly at first. Then, you embrace it. You crave the BEING. You look for ways to stop DOING all the time so there is more time to JUST BE.

With my graphic design background, I naturally look for white space. This white space is the place on the page where your eyes can rest. You can breathe there. I invite you to look for white space in your own life. Where can you breathe? If you can't find any room, you need to look even closer and see what needs to go. Natural white space in your day will allow you to just BE.

For me, it looks like quiet mornings with a cup of coffee, enjoying nature. It's my time to regroup and just BE. No hurry. I had to give up my morning rush, though. Rush, rush, rush. Go go go. It was exhausting and I was exhausted.

Last winter the polar vortex swirled around Central Indiana where I live. As the days grew shorter, so did my patience. I would hear God says to me, "*Be Still* and Know." I thought, "I am being still, but I don't KNOW what you are doing!" Soon I realized that I didn't need to know what He was doing. I had to make the concerted effort to *Be Still*. And, honestly, if you can't *Be Still* with yourself and slow down, you can pretty much guarantee that eventually God will put something in your path to make you still!

I was completely exhausted but continued to press my body and schedule beyond healthy parameters. God was trying to get my attention. Again, I say, if you don't force yourself to slow down, God will! I quit one of my part-time jobs and began hiring help for my marketing company. I cut back on all volunteerism except that which allowed me to be with my two high school-aged boys. The rest of it was out. My friends were curious and rather stunned at what I was doing. Frankly, so was I! But I knew my life depended on it. My marriage needed work, but first I knew I needed to work on me. After that I could assess better if the marriage could continue.

Well-meaning friends would ask me, "What are you doing?" I honestly didn't have an answer. I wasn't *doing* anything. I was *being*. By the way, we are not human-doings. We are human-beings. It was the start of something beautiful for me to realize that. I didn't have to DO-DO-DO all the time. I could just BE. It was beautiful and freeing!

The pressures of the outside world melted away as I embraced this new way of life. I followed my guidance every moment and got STILL. Being Still for me meant to slow down my life, cut out activities, and at times, sit on the couch and stare out the window like the children in *The Cat and The Hat Comes Back*!

This simple, deliberate act of Being Still became a daily ritual that I relish even today. I can't explain it, but in the stillness, I began to:

- Be present.
- Enjoy each moment at a deeper level.
- Feel feelings and release pent up frustrations.
- Reconnect to the God spark inside of myself.
- Have visions of angels.
- Trust and honor myself.
- Know that I was ENOUGH just as I am.
- Feel centered and energized to fulfill my soul's purpose.
- Hear God clearer.

Without being still we stumble through the noise. Without being still we take guesses at where we should be next. Without being still we don't honor ourselves or our true calling.

A few years ago I switched to wearing silver and white gold jewelry, having shunned my usual gold. In some recent work with a mentor, Liana Chaouli, I put a gold necklace on but it didn't feel right, and I quickly took it off. As I held the necklace, it brought tears to my eyes for no apparent reason and sent me into a tailspin! I began to do what I encourage you to do: sit with it. Let come up whatever needs to come up. I asked myself, what is it about this necklace that was upsetting me? Almost immediately, I realized the *gold* represented my gold wedding ring and love. Which now was gone after the divorce.

As I dug even deeper, the gold necklace reminded me of lost love. Both my parents and grandparents expressed their love for one another through jewelry—normally gold. One Christmas in particular, my Grandfather presented my Grandmother with a beautiful gold brooch of two geese, stating his love for her while making the comparison that geese mate for life. A simple gold necklace changed my life that afternoon. I was able to release the feeling of lost love in my own life by noticing and taking the time to dig into the real meaning of my tears. But first I had to *Be Still* and feel.

If we choose to pay attention to our soul's calling, there will be always be moments such as mine with the gold necklace. These are the moments that stop us in our tracks. We get to decide whether we're going to continue numbing ourselves with more unimportant activities or if we are going to step up and observe what is happening in our lives. As we observe, we can feel the emotions that are attached to various moments, release them, and move on from a stronger point.

We are all so busy in our lives. Too busy, perhaps. When I made the effort to slow down and reevaluate my life, miracles began to arrive by the handful. In the stillness, I became more aware of the unseen world around me. God and His angels were guiding my every step. Every word. Every intention. I felt supported and loved. All of sudden, I had more time for my children. One-on-one, face-to-face real talk time to connect with the kids and friends. Meaningful conversations emerged, not only the to-do list for the day. Peace overflowed out of me from my time of stillness. An inner-knowing burst forth, giving me confidence in my decisions.

Mother Teresa described this quietness well saying:

> I'm a little pencil in the hand of a writing God, who is sending a love letter to the world. God cannot be found in noise and restlessness. God is the friend of silence. See how nature – trees, flowers, grass – grows in silence; see the stars, the moon and the sun, how they move in silence... We need silence to be able to touch the soul.

Tiffany began her stillness practice by embarking on a VIP Retreat with me. Fed up with her crazy, busy, out-of-control life, Tiffany hopped on a plane last minute and flew to a beautiful island where I was working with ladies one-on-one.

Exhausted and depleted, she was working over sixty hours a week and raising young children with her husband. She knew something needed to change and this retreat was her catalyst.

From the moment she arrived, Tiffany was able to completely relax and welcome the stillness. Her entire body began to breathe deeply again as she came alive with excitement for her life. In the stillness, Tiffany began to connect to a part of her that she hadn't listened to in a long time. It was the part that she shoved down and out of her way so she could get her work done. This work was an amazing business she had created. Her head began spinning months earlier when her dream business she had created began to grow rapidly. Although thrilled, her family and especially her own sense of self were suffering. She felt like she was riding on a runaway train.

In the stillness at the VIP retreat, Tiffany remembered why she had created this business in the first place. To fit into her life, not take it over. She reorganized her priorities, putting taking care of herself first and foremost and her family second. She committed to a food detox to help her feel her best. Tiffany also began restructuring her life to be filled with love, fun, and a balanced amount of work, all through embracing stillness.

Samantha took a different approach to her stillness. Her approach was a gradual moving away from the busyness of her out-of-control life. She dipped her toes in the Being Still camp much slower than Tiffany, but it was perfect for her. When she got still and quiet she began to recognize she was ENOUGH, and felt excited to step into her soul's purpose. She began saying no to Mr. Wrong to allow Mr. Right to enter through the front door, in his perfect timing.

It took her over a year to weed out negative friends and work situations in her life. This also included a move to an entirely new state. As she continued practicing stillness, Samantha's fears surrounding money began to rear their ugly head. She didn't run from them this time. She welcomed them, recognized them, stayed aware of the fears, and let them come up — one by one. Samantha knew feeling and naming the fear would allow it to dissipate. She continues today to work with these difficult issues in the stillness, as layer upon layer are peeled away.

Jennifer is only beginning to peel away the layers of anger and resentment as she becomes STILL. It seems these awry feelings are arising as quickly as the Titanic sank. After years of stuffing them down with food, activities, and drama, Jennifer is now mature and feels safe being STILL to embrace these difficult feelings. Like Samantha, in the stillness, she is learning to allow the feelings to come up and dissipate layer after layer.

When Amber left her fast-paced big city life for her STILLNESS weekend VIP retreat with me, she had a transformational experience like no other. She was able to let go of her need to lead and control the things she couldn't change. In the stillness, Amber felt safe and allowed herself to feel the emotions that were coming up for her. She cleared some old and deep wounds that had held her back. And, like the others, when those feelings moved on through, what was left behind was an extraordinary gift of presence, clear thinking, and excitement to serve her soul's purpose.

Now, it's your turn. Find a comfy spot to relax. *Be Still.* Next time you are enjoying your *white space* time, ask yourself these questions:

- What can you give up Doing so you can BE?
- What are you hoping for? For yourself? For your business/work? Your family?
- Can you let go of YOUR timing for the PERFECT time?
- What are you feeling in this moment? Can you name it?
- What are you looking at?
- Can you feel your God spark inside of you?

After you welcome stillness into your life, you too will begin to gradually experience moments of bliss, overcome with thankfulness, appreciation and love. You may also begin to be more present in your life, know you are ENOUGH, and hear God clearer.

I'm finishing this chapter after hearing I have Hashimoto's disease — when your own immune system attacks your thyroid — causing all kinds of havoc in many systems in your body. I wonder if the outcome would have been different if I hadn't pushed myself for so many years. Regardless, I'm welcoming it as a wake-up call to take even better care of myself. I'm prepared to embrace this new normal and honor myself in a more deliberate way. Now, my quality of life depends on it.

To *Be Still* is only the beginning of this adventure of setting your spark of hope on fire. In the next chapter we will learn how to put to rest the mind chatter that holds us back.

SILENCE THE
MIND CHATTER

*"Our thoughts are just a story our
mind tells us."* — Romina Avila

Recently I saw an interview with the lead singer of the band Train, Patrick Monahan, who talked about being in therapy and how his therapist pointed out that in our human psyche we always have two voices we can choose to listen to. One he referred to as the angel. From that one therapy session he wrote the moving song, *Calling All Angels*.

This song reminds me as well to call on my angels. In the past, I didn't even think of asking God and his angels for help. Now, it's a part of my every day. They are with me every step. Sometimes, they help me get out of bed when I haven't slept particularly well. They guide me to the places I need to go, and people I need to talk to. I ask for their support and assistance in healing, send them ahead of me to places I'm going, and call them in to carry myself and loved ones to safety when traveling. When I remember to ask for help, my angels are ALWAYS there. They especially help me to decipher the annoying inner critic.

I want to resolve for you once and for all that you do not have to believe every single thought in your head. Our minds are constantly chatting. Some call it mind chatter. Others, monkey mind. Others may even call it the devil! Regardless, this nonstop babble going on in our minds is always going to be there. I want you to know that you do not have to believe it. You get to choose what you *listen* to!

The problem with believing the non-stop mind chatter is it can take us down faster than a punch in the stomach. We listen to this mind chatter over and over tell us: you are stupid, you are ugly, you will never amount to anything, you will never be paid a fair wage, you don't deserve more, you are not enough, you are pathetic. You can't write a book. Who do you think you are? No one wants to hear what you have to say! You begin to believe it. It's all you know. Soon, your self-esteem and self-worth are so far in the dumps you can hardly see over the mound of lies.

Mind chatter can be relentless and just about drive you nuts, until you're able to recognize it for what it is… just chatter. I love the definition of chatter… purposeless or foolish talk. That's exactly what goes on in most of our heads daily. Foolish talk. No purpose to it.

At an early age, I would hear over and over from influential adults and other children alike… you're fat, you're ugly, you're stupid, and you're worthless. Over time, they didn't even have to say it; I would repeat it in my head myself. That's all I heard. All I knew.

Once in high school a teacher threw chalk at me for answering a question incorrectly, yelling I was stupid in the front of the class. Like many high-schoolers, my self-esteem was already fragile, let alone to be verbally beaten up in front of my peers. The teacher may have meant it to be funny but to me there was no one laughing, especially me. The most frustrating part for me was my guidance counselor refused to even acknowledge that what the teacher did was wrong, again reinforcing to me that I was the issue. Such a wakeup call to those of us who do teach about the impact of our words and actions decades later.

When I began to *Be Still*, the mind chatter increased even more. But this time, I was quiet enough to *hear* it, be aware of it, and start questioning it myself. That's another benefit of Being Still – you are slowed down so you can be aware of what is really happening in your world. You begin to notice. Inevitably, the chatter volume will increase for you as well. That's okay. Welcome it. Let it happen.

Numerous studies have proven for every thought we think there is a chemical reaction that sends messages throughout our body. I knew if I began sending positive messages to my body, it would eventually reflect that cheerful image. For example, often dread would come over me regarding an upcoming event. I would begin to feel listless, tired, angry, and even frustrated thinking about what may or may not happen.

As I began noticing the negative thoughts, I would reframe them to envision my ideal outcome. I would focus on the best case scenario, not the worst. It wasn't long before my mood began improving with a brighter outlook. With each reframe of the negative thoughts, my energy even seemed to magically increase.

As you hear the mind chatter speaking foolish talk, acknowledge it. Experts on this topic differ on their opinions... some say to ignore it and let it pass. Others encourage you to recognize it for what it is – foolish talk – and even tell yourself the opposite. For example, if your mind chatter may repeatedly tell you, "You are fat. I can't believe you're even thinking of eating today," in your stillness, you become aware of the thought that is running in your mind and turn it around and say back to yourself, "I am beautifully and wonderfully made. I am healthy, healed, and whole. Everything I eat benefits me." I recommend using the method that works best for you.

For whatever reason, I never understood for years that the talk inside my head wasn't necessarily true. I can decide whether or not to believe it. When I realized this, it was life changing! I didn't have to believe everything my own head was screaming at me! I could sit back and let it talk all it wanted while I chose what was true and what wasn't.

Once I became aware of this 24/7 recording going on in the background of my mind, my life gradually opened up to new possibilities. I began to see clearly how my thoughts (consciously or not) were creating my future. I was able to recognize ahead of time when I was headed onto a downward slippery slope and chose to change the recording playing. Eventually, my spark inside began to light up with excitement for life. My self-esteem increased. Depression lifted. Confidence soared. I began to believe in myself and feel a purpose for living. I was coming alive day by day as I changed the recording of the mind chatter.

A Type-A super smart client, Michael, recently came to me for help with a recurring mind chatter loop. His chatter was sending him onto a slippery slope of hopelessness. The same messages were replaying over and over in his mind. Experiencing frustration and aggravation, he couldn't break the loop. When we talked, he acknowledged that he was well aware of the mind chatter, but didn't know how to stop the maddening thoughts. Michael was partially trying the second method of being aware of the mind chatter but he wasn't able to turn the thoughts into something positive yet. He was trying to make sense of the foolish talk when there was no sense to be made! So, we tried a different approach. I encouraged him to ignore it instead! Sometimes when one method doesn't work, you try the other one. And, this was the best solution for Michael.

When the thoughts entered his mind, he was aware but allowed them to pass on through and got busy doing something he enjoyed. Next time I talked to him, he was relaxed, energized, and thrilled that he could enjoy his life again without the same maddening, debilitating thoughts replaying in his mind.

My client Jennifer, previously mentioned in the *Be Still* chapter, also struggles with a mind that doesn't stop chattering, even to the point of not sleeping at night. Sometimes, she pushes herself to stay super busy so she doesn't have to slow down and *hear* her chatter.

Instead of ignoring the thoughts, like Michael, Jennifer embraced reframing the thoughts. In the stillness, she began to hear the thoughts that were coming up. Mostly thoughts were of fear and frustration, reminding her of all the things she should be doing differently or better at work and at home. She was allowing these thoughts to run her life. They were beginning to take over her life, even causing illness in her body, when she came to me for assistance. I explained how for every thought we think there is a chemical reaction that is sent out into our body. No wonder her body was reacting to these negative thoughts!

As Jennifer acknowledged and reframed the recordings into a positive light, her fear subsided, confidence soared, and she began feeling peace over her body. I suspect the more positive talk sent out happy chemicals to her body to help it calm down and heal.

Nowadays, I have quite a different relationship with my own mind chatter. Oh, it's always there. I normally acknowledge it, decide for myself whether it's truth and Christ-like (or from the angels, like Patrick Monahan says) and then choose to let it pass on through or accept it. When you choose to not believe all the foolish talk the chatter is telling you, you can begin to tell it the truth and have an entirely different outlook on life. In the next chapter, we will tap into what comes after you get still and *Silence the Mind Chatter*, and that is *Mindfulness and Meditation*.

I encourage you to begin to listen to the voices in your own head. I suspect if you're suffering from low self-worth, you've been listening to a voice that tells you such. Now, it's time to relax and let that negative mind chatter pass right on through or reframe the message. And, *Calling All Angels* isn't a bad idea either!

MINDFULNESS AND MEDITATION

*"Be happy in the moment, that's enough.
Each moment is all we need, not more."* – Mother Teresa

In *The Mindful Way through Depression*, Mark Williams wrote:

> Start living right here, in each present moment. When we
> stop dwelling on the past or worrying about the future,
> we're open to rich sources of information we've been
> missing out on—information that can keep us out of the
> downward spiral and poised for a richer life.

Everywhere I go people want to push on me their way of being
mindful and meditating. There are even proper ways to breathe
now. I can never seem to do anything right by the experts'
standards. Well-meaning teachers will insist their way is the only
way and I'm doing it all wrong. Nothing is more frustrating to me!

Let me begin by saying I'm not an expert on this topic. However, I
know what has worked for me, and what is right for me and my life.

For our purposes, the right way is whatever way feels right to you! Just as there are many roads that lead to the same destination, so it is the same for these hot topics.

There are hundreds, if not thousands of books and articles written on mindfulness, meditation, and breathing. I'm not even sure that I can do it justice condensing it into one small chapter. What I invite you to do though, is begin. Begin a practice of learning about these subjects and becoming aware of the huge impact and benefit they can have on your life. Learn the basics. Don't shy away from meditating thinking it's something woo-woo.

For decades, I was told by the church not to meditate or do yoga because those were against God. That's very odd, because when I'm practicing meditation, I feel closer to God than EVER. Meditating allows me to connect to God on a level that can only be done one-on-one. For me, prayer is when I'm doing all the talking to God. In meditation, I finally get quiet enough to HEAR. I can clearly hear what God is saying to me!

When I began embracing *Mindfulness and Meditation*, I felt an all-around peace. My thoughts were clearer; my energy was focused. Life had an easier ebb and flow. Messages were crystal clear. I began to sense, see and hear angels. The more I surrendered my agenda, my expectations, and my ego, God was able to speak through me in a powerful way.

I don't know what to call *it* or label it. In the church and in healing circles, it's often called *speaking in tongues* or *Angel Speak*. All I know is that this beautiful language that pours through me moves mountains. People are healed. They have said they feel lighter, with a skip in their step. Others feel like they have just had a chiropractic adjustment and rest is usually in order while they assimilate whatever healing God orchestrated. What it does for others, it does for me as well. All because I began to meditate and be open to God's possibilities for my life.

My family and friends could tell something was different, but couldn't quite put their fingers on it. Although some may argue this point, I even became much more patient! I started enjoying the little things in life. Even doing the dishes became an enjoyable activity!

Practicing *Mindfulness and Meditation* will allow you to look at your life from a new perspective. From the inside, out. Easier said than done on some days, but so rewarding. It starts with being still, quieting the mind chatter and next, digging deeper.

Embarking on this sort of practice can seem daunting. I want to take the scary out of it for you and give you a simple guide to get started. Often the words, *Mindfulness and Meditation*, are used interchangeably. Part of the confusion is that they both have numerous meanings. However, in fact, they are quite different. For our purposes, I'll share a simple way to differentiate the two.

– Mindfulness –

Mindfulness means being aware or focusing on something intently. Being in the present moment. During meditation, you are being mindful. But you can also be mindful throughout your day during various activities, such as: during driving or when you're eating, playing with your kids or talking on the phone with a friend. Mindfulness has been embraced by millions of people. You find it in the boardroom (Google), the classroom (various school districts), and even our government.

Here are some top ways to be mindful throughout your day:

- Eat slowly and with focus. Enjoy each bite along with your company and the atmosphere you are experiencing.
- Focus on the person who is in front of you as you are talking to them.
- Be 100% present no matter what you are doing — writing an email, texting, driving, working out, walking on the beach, eating, doing the dishes, talking to your children, playing. Whatever you do — do it with all of you!

According to *Doing and Being: Mindfulness, Health, and Quiet Ego Characteristics among Buddhist Practitioners*, the 2011 research article that published the survey results in the Journal of Happiness Studies [12(4): 575-589], there were five key ways that mindfulness training increased physical and mental health.

1. It strengthened the immune system and physiological responses to stress and negative emotions.
2. It improved social relationships with family and strangers.
3. It reduced stress, depression, and anxiety and increased well-being and happiness.
4. It increased openness to experience, conscientiousness, and agreeableness and reduced negative associations with neuroticism.
5. It led to greater psychological mindfulness, which included an awareness that is clear, non-conceptual, and flexible; a practical stance toward reality; and present attention to the individual's consciousness and awareness.

– Meditation –

The official definition of Meditation is to engage in contemplation or reflection, usually with a focused mental intent or a single point of reference. According to *Psychology Today*:

> It can involve focusing on the breath, on bodily sensations, or on a word or phrase known as a mantra. In other words, meditation means turning your attention away from distracting thoughts and focusing on the present moment.

For myself, each day begins and ends with prayer and meditation. When I first began meditating, I would use a guided meditation. It would help me relax while staying focused on the nothingness I sought. As my skill increased in this area, I was able to take a few deep breathes while dropping into the space of no-space in almost an instant. When I'm seeking guidance on important issues in my life, meditation is always my first stop. I invite you as well to look within your own heart for God's direction for your life.

Let's practice being in the present moment.

While you are Being Still you will most likely begin to hear some mind chatter. It's nothing that you need to concern yourself with. Choose to let it pass on through along with your endless to-do list. Instead, focus on the love in your heart. That is your true essence.

Don't give up. Sit and enjoy that white space in your day. At first it may feel awkward and non-productive. Acknowledge that's how you feel and move on.

Next, I want you to close your eyes and breathe.

Take a deep breath and feel your breath come up one side of your body. Hold for four seconds. Release slowly, feeling it go down the other side of your body. Do this three times.

Now, envision your heart. Put your attention on your heart. Can you feel it pumping? Can you feel the love inside of it? Imagine the love growing inside of you. What does it feel like? Scan the rest of your body. What are you feeling? Are there any emotions that are coming up? If so, feel them. One by one. One by one. One by one. Acknowledge them. Name the feelings. Let them pass on through.

Shed a tear, if you must. Let it flow through you. Let whatever must come up for the day, come up and out. Let it flow. Move out of your body. Feel your body feeling lighter and lighter as emotion after emotion is dealt with and moved through. Continue to acknowledge all that needs to come up for the day. Thank your body for what it is doing and processing for you. Encourage yourself for the day.

What can you tell yourself that will help you today? For example, it's going to be a great day. Or, I am healthy, healed and whole.

Set your intention for the day. What do you want to get done? What do you want to do today that will make it a GREAT day? Do you need to call anyone? How can you show up for your life today? Set that intention.

While you're still *inside*, imagine yourself standing on the green grass, and feel the grass on your bare feet. Feel it for about four seconds and then open your eyes.

What you have experienced is a meditation. Meditation is not some rah rah woo woo new age thing. It is real. Try it, then tell me you didn't feel better!

I encourage all my clients to take time each day to meditate. It's too important to miss.

The benefits of *Mindfulness and Meditation* are mind-blowing. Studies have shown in meditation, EVERY cell in the body is filled with more energy which results in joy, peace, and enthusiasm.

Specifically, here are a few other benefits:

- Reduces stress/Decreases anxiety.
- Adds clarity and peace of mind.
- Lowers high blood pressure.
- Decreases tension in the body.
- Increases serotonin production.
- Improves the immune system.
- Increases the energy level.
- Improves concentration.
- Encourages healthy lifestyle.
- Problems shrink.
- Brings to mind solutions.

The great news about meditation is that the results are cumulative. As you embrace the practice, the benefits will add up.

After some initial hesitation, Tiffany relaxed while hearing the guided words of a one-on-one meditation with me. There were tears, laughs, even surprise as she melted into the words and images that God was showing her. As she sprung up from this new experience, she smiled with a sense of awe she had never experienced before. In the days following, Tiffany still remembered vividly the clear messages she received in her meditation and the calmness she felt. Feeling such enormous benefits, she makes time almost daily now for a shorter meditation.

Jennifer was also new to meditation but eager to learn. She began with small amounts of time – Five to ten minutes here and there. Usually she used a guided meditation from the internet. Other times, she put on some soft music to play while she quieted her mind. After a few weeks, Jennifer began to notice subtle changes in how she reacted to events in her life. She was more patient with her husband and children. She didn't seem as angry at the little mishaps during the day, either. Overall, Jennifer felt happier and more at peace, which she attributed to the cumulative effects of meditation.

Evan was seasoned at meditation but had never used it for anything other than his personal life. When I began working with him, we focused on a guided meditation to take his business to the next level. This was a remarkable experience for him that he reverts back to even months later. He was able to see the health of his business. He gleaned information that helped him in restructuring his business to be more profitable while helping his clients at an even deeper level.

Like Jennifer, Tiffany, and Evan, I can't imagine my life without meditation. My life has transformed partly due to this one practice alone. It quickly centers me and provides a reset anytime, anywhere. This, too, could be your go-to for reducing the stress in your daily life.

Where meditating is generally a quiet inner focus with our eyes closed, going outside in nature asks us to open our eyes to take in the beauty surrounding us. In the next chapter, we will look more closely at the benefits of spending time outdoors.

I can't promise that you will begin to see angels or speak unknown healing words; that's between you and God. At first you may see progress in terms of physical relaxation and emotional calmness. Later you may notice other, more subtle changes. Some of the most important benefits of meditation make themselves known gradually over time and are not dramatic or easily observed. Persist in your practice and you will find that meditation is a means of freeing yourself from the worries that gnaw at you. Then you are free to experience the joy of being fully present, here and now.

THE HEALING
EFFECTS OF NATURE

"Nature itself is the best medicine." – Hippocrates

Do you ever stand at the ocean's edge? Relish in the crashing waves? Or perhaps the beautiful mountains of Sedona? Maybe hiking is your thing. How do you feel when you are in the midst of the beauty? Balanced? Centered? Relaxed?

As I write this chapter, I'm enjoying the view of this beautiful Japanese garden at the Four Season's Westlake Village, California. As I walked the gardens, I came alive. The worries of the day melted away and I soaked up the beauty of this incredible space.

Often, on a daily basis, we're handling life as if it comes at us, fast and furious. We spend our days putting out fires which causes many other emotional, physical, and psychological issues.

We can't sleep. We clench our teeth. We forgot to breathe. We forget who we are.

The stress from the pressure cooker of life increases in the body and we become anxious, angry, and can even sink into depression. All this from our everyday life of living!

The past decade has been very stressful in my personal life. Life events such as family member deaths, surgeries, divorce, computers stolen, becoming an empty nester, moving from the family home, illnesses, floods, and more have turned my life inside out. Nature was an integral part of healing me through this difficult period.

As stress mounted in my life, I knew it was time for me to take a different route. I was at a point in my life where my health challenges and past traumas were affecting my daily quality of living. I became concerned as the winter months in the Midwest were approaching. I tend towards depression and Indiana's cloudy winter days combined with cold temperatures and snow were not sitting well with me. Thus, I made a decision to become a snowbird and flew south to the ocean!

Typically, a snowbird is a retiree who chooses to avoid the snow or cold by living in a warmer temperature climate for a few months out of each year. I've always been drawn to various beaches for short vacations so this was an easy decision for me, as I knew it would provide a natural location that would support my healing. Two solid months of rest, relaxation, and being.

The daily walks on the beach, viewing sunsets over the ocean, and relaxing on the Island became an integral part of my routine that supported my body as it healed. When I walked on the sand, I envisioned my past traumas being taken out into the ocean, never to be seen again. Each step meant something else that was holding me back from the life I really wanted to live was let go. Emotions were released from the deepest of cells in my body. Some days I would walk with tears of sorrow. Other days, tears of joy.

Regardless of the reason, the ocean and sunsets provided a background of beauty and support that assisted me in a myriad of ways.

Playing in nature helped me to:

- Mend my broken heart.
- Release self-limiting beliefs that were holding me back.
- Release old patterns and open up to unlimited possibilities.
- Reconnect to my soul's desire to enjoy the beauty of life.
- Reconnect with my own spark of hope.
- Renew my commitment to my own self-care and self-worth.
- Renew my spiritual connection.
- Renew my commitment to pursue my greatest dreams.

All that because I walked along the ocean's edge and viewed the sunsets any chance I could get! Author Wallace J. Nichols wrote about this fascinating connection in *Blue Mind: The Surprising*

Science That Shows How Being Near, In, On, or Under Water Can Make You Happier, Healthier, More Connected, and Better at What You Do. He said, "Like a child depends upon its mother, humans have always depended upon nature for our survival. And just as we intuitively love our mothers, we are linked to nature physically, cognitive and emotionally."

In the early 80s, a researcher in Paoli, Pennsylvania collected information about patients who had undergone gallbladder surgery over a nine-year period. The research looked at the difference in patients' recoveries based on the difference of one patient's hospital bed facing a brick wall and another facing a group of trees. Apart from their differing views, the rooms were identical. The results were not surprising. On average, those who faced the brick wall needed an extra day to recover before returning home. They were far more depressed and experienced more pain. Meanwhile, very few of the patients who looked out onto the trees required more than a single dose of strong painkillers during the middle part of their stay, whereas those facing the wall required two or even three doses.

Studies repeatedly have shown that hanging out in nature can lower blood pressure, reduce anxiety, relieve stress, sharpen mental states, and even help those suffering from ADHD disorders, depression, addictions, insomnia, stress and more. Nature tends to bring out the best in each of us. It soothes, heals, restores, and even connects us.

It's amazing what being out in nature does for people. Years ago my older brother had a landscape business and planted hundreds of trees in his backyard. He told me watching them grow was his church.

Recently, I spent several days hiking the beautiful Mount Shasta in Northern California. This trip in nature was a last minute add-on to a week of non-stop meetings. The quietness of the forest almost immediately reset my body and mind. Hiking seems to be very healing for me. With each foot in front of the other, my mind wandered, but, mostly, I tried to *Be Still* and do a walking meditation to keep silent. I wanted to be present. Soak in every noise, every tree rustle. Hear every step and each bird chirping. It didn't take long before I had forgotten all about the Los Angeles traffic!

While hiking uphill and dodging boulders in the pathway, I also noticed different emotions would surface. At times I would laugh but mostly I was crying! As I let the emotions pass on through without trying to figure them out or judge them, I felt stronger. Even my hiking steps changed. Instead of walking around the boulders in the pathway, I began to step ON THEM for leverage to go higher, further, faster! This is a lesson from nature for us as well. Step on the boulders in our life! Those things that seemingly are in our way may actually be there to launch us even further at a faster rate. Instead of trying to side-step the obstacle, embrace it, put your foot on it and let it give you a stronger leverage to propel you into your future.

For whatever reason, hiking and being out in nature for me seem to escalate this sort of healing by processing emotions. By the time I left Mount Shasta, I was a different person—centered, grounded, relaxed and quiet. What better place to release past hurts and sadness than surrounded by God's beauty?

Samantha has a very stressful job in the corporate world with an unending inbox and staring at a computer screen daily. Even though lunch is brought in daily for staff members, Samantha normally chooses to pack her lunch and sit outside to enjoy it in the quiet. Usually right after she eats, she takes a short walk around the block before she returns to her desk, unending inbox, and computer screen. Samantha says that since she started this practice, her mental clarity and focus are stronger than ever, especially in the afternoon when most people's energy drops.

If you're a person who doesn't normally spend time outdoors, I challenge you to start with a fifteen minute walk outside every evening. Notice how you feel. Do you feel more centered? Balanced? Energized? Focused? Just notice and follow those feelings of bliss.

In the next chapter, we're going to talk about setting up your life for success. Being in nature is an integral part of that success and can also help facilitate this difficult step in renewing your commitment to yourself.

There are hundreds of other studies outlining the benefits of spending time outdoors. What is important to note from these studies is the overall consensus is... spend time outdoors, with others, every day. This will provide the well-needed restorative experience your body craves to be in balance. And, isn't that what a family beach vacation does? Soak up the grass, flowers, sun, waves, mountains, trees, rocks, streams...let them balance you and reconnect with the true you, which is complete self-love!

SLEEP, SCHEDULES, AND SURROUNDINGS

"You should deeply care about what you think, what you want, what you need, and what makes you feel happy. Just as important, you should have plans and routines in place that allow you to do all these things and care for yourself in general." – Brendon Burchard

Success reminds me of watching my boys in the Avon (High School) Marching Black & Gold Band, aka AMB&G. They would work for hours and hours on the same thirty seconds of the show. Over and over and over. It would be perfect. Their bodies would remember what to do even when they were exhausted. They could do it in their sleep.

During the same hours the kids were on the field, parents and other employees were stocking Gatorade and energy bars for competitions, building and sewing props, writing music, cleaning and fixing instruments, polishing shoes, matching socks, ironing uniforms, preparing first aid kits, and more. All the parts work together – the staff (paid and volunteer), students, and parents blend their time and talents into a six-month season and hundreds of hours on the field. Even when the student was at home, rest and nutrition were still a high priority to keep their bodies functioning at a high level. When it was show time, 300 students of the AMB&G took the field doing their thing like a well-oiled machine. The 3-time Grand National Champions and 11-time Indiana State Winning trophies tell the story of success.

What would happen if the AMB&G didn't have their program set up for pristine success? For starters, they wouldn't have won all the awards and accolades that they have. There would also be complete chaos at performances. Students would run into each other on the field. There's no telling what would happen off the field with the parents and staff! Instruments would be broken; students would be hungry, thirsty, and tired. Uniforms would be wrinkled and ripped. These are just a few issues lack of organization and structure can cause.

In our own lives, incomplete structures create chaos, as well. We would fly by the seat of our pants when it came to our daily responsibilities. Maybe dishes wouldn't get done. But then again, maybe we wouldn't even have groceries to cook and would need to eat most of our meals out. Forget beds ever being made or home projects ever getting done. Eating healthy and working out would be something that would never enter your mind because there wouldn't be *time* for such splurges. You most likely would sleep in because you stayed up late watching TV; there was no schedule the next day but you always felt like you couldn't get it all done.

Your surroundings would be filled with clutter, unpacked boxes, memories of unmet dreams, and stuff that no longer represented you. This *stuff* would hold you back from moving forward in your life without you even knowing it.

I often wondered what it would take to live life like a well-oiled machine—smooth, a daily flow, seldom rushed, enjoyed, not endured, full of beauty, love, and adventure. For me, I saw that it would take a life embedded with structures in the background that kept me going even when I didn't *feel* like it.

Structures provide an arrangement for the parts of our lives that we need to set us up for success to be that well-oiled machine on a daily basis. Being the creative, multi-faceted, spiritual woman that I am who wants to go with the flow without expectation or judgement, I resist structure sometimes. Ok, most of the time! It's not that I don't desire it. I do. I love to be organized and have systems in place but I resist structuring my day because I want to be open to where or what God is leading me to do in the moment. I already have enough material to write a whole different book on being led by God in the moment, but for now, suffice it to say, every day is an adventure!

These days, in order to run a successful business and write powerful books that will help people know they are enough, I've merged my openness to God with a spirit-led schedule and integrated my daily responsibilities that work for me. Yearly goals down to daily schedules are prayed over and tweaked as I'm led.

This partnership has set my life and business up for success while still allowing me to be open to God's flow. Three of the main areas that helped me to oil my machine called *life* were sleep, schedules, and surroundings.

– Sleep –

After several bouts of mononucleosis, adrenal exhaustion and now thyroid disease, I have learned the importance of sleep. I'm a slow learner! When my body doesn't get the proper amount of sleep, you can bet that nothing else in my body or day is going to work properly either! And, for you, I suspect it's the same. Having a great day on Tuesday actually starts Monday night, by getting to bed at an hour that sets you up for success.

Although during the last decade I have struggled to sleep at night, a few months ago I went through a period of time where I slept ten hours a night plus a nap! When I was awake I would go for a short walk and worked as best I could. I honored this unusual schedule my body was craving, while, of course, hoping it wouldn't last too long! I was beginning to feel guilty. Why? Because that's what we are conditioned to feel if we're not performing at optimum levels on a regular basis.

I say that's all fine and good but when our bodies are suffering through our pushing, we're not doing anyone any favors. We get run down. Exhausted. Cranky! That long period of rest for me came after months of a very stressful time in my life. My body was demanding a BREAK!

Our bodies are these beautiful masterpieces.... even intricate tapestries, if you will, that need to be loved and treated with kid gloves. Especially the older we get. When we're younger we can get away with less sleep, even more junk food. But as we age, we are not quite as resilient. It's important to really connect to your body on a daily, almost hourly basis. Listen to what it's trying to tell you. Don't ignore the signs before it's screaming at you that something more serious is wrong.

Daily life can be stressful. The best thing we can do is to honor our bodies on a regular basis as we ride the waves of life. That's true self-love.

I remind you today to honor your body. Become aware of its need to REST and offer it what it is asking. You will be amazed at the outcome. Whether your body is calling for a good night's sleep or three weeks of Rip Van Winkle kind of sleep, you will be amazed at the outcome. When it's *done* over sleeping, we will naturally come back into balance.

My client, Sally, was struggling to get to sleep and stay asleep at night. She was menopause-aged with fluctuating hormones that were causing a massive disruption in her sleep cycle. As it lingered, it began causing issues for her during the day. She was listless when she should have been wide awake. She was depending on caffeine to keep up with her busy schedule, which was only making her feeling worse. Feeling defeated and frustrated with herself, I encouraged her to get a full panel of hormone tests and begin working with a physician to balance her hormones as well as add in a natural sleep supplement.

A few weeks later, I saw Sally smiling from ear to ear because she was finally sleeping soundly and deeply, while her body was adjusting to the naturally balanced hormones.

– Schedules –

Aristotle wrote, "We are what we repeatedly do." As I mentioned earlier, I knew intuitively that schedules are important, but I resisted following one! I would set them, but not follow them, then beat myself up for not following the schedule that I set!

I've heard Jana Kingsford say, "Balance is not something you find, it's something you create." To balance means something is used to produce equilibrium. In our daily lives, there are not just two things we need to do every day to balance the scale. Instead, we juggle hundreds of activities each month that need to weigh evenly on our own scale of daily life. Instead of thinking that you need to *balance* your life, envision each activity you partake in as a spoke on a wheel, a piece of your life that needs oil to run smoothly.

In our case of daily responsibilities and living life with the goal of ease and flow, to balance our lives, in my opinion, means to fill our lives with activities that blend together all that we need to live a full life. Scheduling a good amount of sleep, work, play, relationship connections, healthy meals, and workouts every day sets you up to skyrocket your self-worth and self-love. You are no good to anyone if all you do is work constantly. Life is about living, loving and relationships.

For you, it might mean only working four hours a day. Who says we all have to work forty hours a week? And, why can't that work be done while you're overlooking a beautiful beach or mountain top? Design your life and business around what YOU LOVE. This is self-love... taking care of yourself FIRST and then adding other important routines into your schedule. It should never be the other way around.

I ask clients what their morning and evening routines are. They usually look at me with wide eyes because there is no routine! I totally get it. I didn't have any problem showing up for other people but I neglected myself. When I began a morning routine it became a sacred time where I showed up for ME. And, what I learned was establishing a routine not only set me up for a successful day but it provided fuel to increase my self-esteem and was an act of self-love. Again, contributing to that well-oiled machine.

Darren Hardy talks about the power of routines in his book, *The Compound Effect*. He says:

A routine is something you do every day without fail, so that eventually, like brushing your teeth or putting on your seatbelt, you do it without conscious thought... To establish profitable and effective routines, you must first decide what behaviors and habits you want to implement.

Think about what YOU need to fuel yourself for the day. For me it was quiet time, coffee, prayer, meditation, and a workout. Write it down in your calendar and commit to yourself. This is a beautiful act of self-love! Daily, I follow my God-guidance in getting things done.

My client Michael, whom I mentioned earlier in the book, schedules his day from sun up till sun down with daily responsibilities and activities and little creative time built in. After getting sick and realizing he was not living his purpose, Michael came to me perplexed on how to infuse creative time for his life's work in a built-in solid schedule. We discussed utilizing a few hours of focused time each day where Facebook, email, and texting would be shut off so he could focus strictly on his creative project. After only a week of this new schedule, Michael was blown away by how much he had accomplished by shutting down the unnecessary for the important creative work he needed to do.

On a daily basis, I'm always asking God and his angels for assistance to get done what I need to get done and to let the rest go. When I do ask, my day falls into place. Maybe not how I would have planned it, but perfect nonetheless. Regardless of the system you use—digital, paper, or a combo, spend some time in prayer asking God for guidance. We all have unique needs and purposes, and we process information differently. No one schedule is perfect for everyone. Let your schedule be set with guidance from the Heavens that propel you to be your best YOU. It's amazing how the important items get done seamlessly while the unimportant fall away. There is even time left at the end of the day for fun!

– Surroundings –

In *The Compound Effect*, Darren Hardy says, "Everyone is affected by three kinds of influences: input (what you feed your mind), associations, (the people with whom you spend time with), and environment (your surroundings)."

Because I'm super sensitive and empathetic, I tend to be a bit picky about my environment, the food I eat, the people I'm around, and what I listen to (or don't listen to). I like things clean and in order, the TV off (generally), and a calm mindset for the day.

I know what feeds my soul and I try every day to do as many of those things as possible that help me feel better. As I already mentioned, this past winter I moved south just to stay warm. I KNEW for me my environment needed to change, even if for a short time.

Recently I downsized, or rather *right-sized*, to a house almost half of what I lived in for twenty-five years. I was in the process of finishing this book, but surrounded by a hundred full boxes and many unfinished projects in the new house. Talk about overwhelmed! Being the determined, resourceful woman that I am, I called in HELP! An angel arrived at my door by the name of Diane Halfman (DianeHalfman.com). She helped me unpack, scale down, clear out over forty years of clutter and put solid structures in place to make that well-oiled machine run pristinely.

I've always been an organized person, loving my label maker, but Diane took it to a level that blew me away! Being organized means having a formal structure, especially to coordinate or carry out widespread activities. This is exactly what I needed her for… to set up my physical space so it will support me to carry out the future activities of my business and life. It was emotional, exhausting, and exhilarating – all at the same time!

In addition to being an expert at evaluating her client's personal environments, Diane Halfman is also an Ultimate Game of Life Coach (TheUltimateGameOfLife.com). She is passionate about connecting and collaborating with others to help them gain clarity on living in their ultimate personal spaces—physically, mentally and spiritually. She moves people from overwhelming circumstances. While she was making magic organizing my belongings, she talked about the Ultimate Environment.

According to the TheUltimateGameOfLife.com website:

Most people think they need more information on how-to create more wealth, create better health, and be happier. There is some truth in the idea that you need to know the proper how-to, because if you are practicing the wrong behavior daily, you are guaranteed a negative result.

The missing element for the 95% who don't succeed is a concept called *The Ultimate Environments of You*. There are 9 Environments that control the way you think, the way you feel, and the way you act. In order to play your biggest game you must understand the environments that are working with you and upgrade the environments that are working against you. When you feel stress, struggle, or delay in reaching your goals, you have most likely created environments that are working against you and your goals, instead of pulling you towards your goals.

Setting these 9 environments up for success is the key to propelling forward in your business and life goals. They include the areas: Self, Spiritual, Relationships, Network, Financial, Physical, Nature, Body, and You. Since the boxes were unpacked and my surroundings were organized, I've been able to focus intently on this important book, without worry.

Natalie came to me frustrated because she wasn't able to make any progress in her home business. Her life's work was full of struggle and blockages, she said. When we began to dismantle her belief system, it was apparent that she really wasn't stuck in her business at all. She was holding tight to the past, all the while trying to move forward. Her house had become a museum, paying homage to the days gone by. I encouraged her to go through each item in the house, especially through her memory albums. Really sitting with them, feeling whatever came up. Holding each item. She asked herself questions like, "Do I really need this? What does it represent to me? Was it important? Is it now important? Do I need it to move forward with me?" Natalie did the hard work required on her surroundings. She said it wasn't easy. As a matter of fact, it was one of the hardest things she has ever done in her life. But well worth it. Clearing her surroundings of the past has allowed her to live in the moment and soar into the future, she says!

When you implement the proper *Sleep, Schedules, and Surroundings* for your life, you will be amazed at the results. Chaos will now be an organized, enjoyable, smooth flow. Your life will move like a well-oiled machine, eager to embrace the present and live out your bravest dream.

After you set yourself up for success in your sleep, schedules and surroundings, you'll feel more equipped to usher in the next chapter's mission to know deep down that you are enough exactly as you are.

Whether we know it or not, our surroundings affect us and our daily work. If you're feeling stuck or not able to move forward in an area of your life, review these environments and, specifically, your surroundings. Take the time to clear out clutter and weed through the past so you can move into your future with ease and flow. Most importantly, know what success means to you. We all have a different idea of what success looks like in our lives. Don't let someone else's viewpoint be yours! Know yourself and you will know what success means to you.

ROCK WHAT YOU'VE GOT

"You are enough. You have nothing to prove to anybody." – Maya Angelou

Dear Body:

I loathe you. I hate that you don't look the way I want you to. That you aren't a perfect size 0. I hate that I push you and push you and you fight me by gaining weight or making my hair fall out. I hate that you aren't perfect. I hate that I have to take care of you and you still don't look like I want you to. It's very frustrating. I hate that you can't or won't do all that I ask. There is so much in my life I want to do and you aren't there for me. Why won't you do what you're supposed to do? How can I love you if you're not perfect?

Sad to say, that was my journal entry only a few years ago. There was no self-love to be found in my life at that time. I may have had this image in my head what a perfect body was, but that wasn't necessarily God's plan. He created each of us perfectly to reflect Him in a specific way. We are meant to be different! Nor are we created to *do* everything.

In the *Introduction* we talked in-depth about self-love. As a reminder, I said:

> Self-love is a gentle acceptance, and unconditional sense of support and caring, and a core of compassion for yourself. It is an abiding willingness to meet your own needs, allow yourself to feel and think whatever you feel and think, and see yourself as essentially worthy, good, valuable, and belonging in the world, deserving of happiness. And, most importantly, you believe you are ENOUGH, as you are. Self-love is developed early in life, and if childhood experiences damage our sense of self significantly, a lack of self-love can hurt us for a lifetime.

Folks who struggle with self-love can't believe they are ENOUGH. No matter how hard they try or how often they hear it from others, they can't seem to believe they are good enough.

A few of the more common characteristics of genuinely low Self-Esteem are:

- You struggle with anger or depression.
- You get frustrated easily.
- You have an eating disorder.
- You may socially withdraw.
- An inability to see yourself *squarely* or to be fair to yourself.
- You can't accept compliments.
- You neglect yourself.

- You treat yourself badly, but not other people.
- You are reluctant to take on challenges.
- You are reluctant to put yourself first.
- You are reluctant to trust your own opinion.
- You expect little out of life for yourself.

Self-esteem is important for many reasons. We need to have a healthy self-esteem because it affects every aspect of our lives. Having a good self-esteem is essential, because:

- Without it, we can crumble and not show up for our life.
- It helps us feel good about our ourselves.
- It gives us courage to try new things.
- It helps us honor and respect ourselves, even when we make mistakes.
- It encourages us to make healthy decisions for our minds and bodies.

All this does not mean that a person with good self-esteem discounts others. Instead, they value themselves and ensure their own feelings or needs are not discounted.

In this chapter, I'd like to offer that you decide for yourself, once and for all, that you are ENOUGH. That's it. ENOUGH. Perfectly, imperfect. Take the pressure off yourself and feel that in your body for a moment. What comes up for you? How does that feel?

Rocking what you've got is SELF-LOVE at its finest! It's about embracing yourself as you are in this moment. Knowing you are ENOUGH. Loving all of you, even if your body doesn't look like OR act like what you think it should. It's about reminding yourself you are worthy and dressing your best each day to reflect your worthiness.

It starts with a mindset of ENOUGH. Instead of beating yourself up with words that put you in a deeper, darker mood and tearing yourself down physically, emotionally and spiritually, I'm encouraging you to be gentle and loving to yourself.

For whatever traumatic reasons, I became disconnected from my body very early in life. Even as young as eight years old, I remember hating my body and wishing I had a different one. I didn't feel loved or that I belonged in my family or anywhere, frankly. Being disconnected also showed up in my life over the years as stress, overwhelm, a sense of emptiness, lack of meaning or purpose, and feeling uncertain about myself.

My inner critic continued to add fuel to the fire. Sad to say, *I am not enough* was my new inner mantra. I grew up with a beautiful dresser and mirror set in my bedroom. Wouldn't really have known it then. I covered the mirror in cardboard so I didn't have to look at myself. I loathed looking at myself in the mirror. I was always wishing I was a different person, different size, different hair, different everything. I didn't believe I was enough. It took years for me to be able to take the cardboard down and actually appreciate my body.

Some days *Rock What You've Got* is still a tough one for me. When I walk on the beach, there are many gals with beautiful buff bodies passing by me. They are probably thirty years younger than me in their itsy-bitsy bikinis. I know we shouldn't compare ourselves with others. I try hard not to, but, we are all human. In the past, I would verbally berate myself, which made me feel even worse. Nowadays is a different story. I embrace my beautiful body and appreciate what it does for me every day.

I encourage you to appreciate who you are right now. Know you are ENOUGH. Right here. Right now. You don't have to be someone you are not. Be the best version of YOU. *Rock What You've Got* is about accepting and loving the body and all of who you are or have in this moment. And, when you love who you are in this moment, you naturally begin to dress to reflect that beautiful inner you and feel rockin'.

Recently a coach of mine was getting ready to present at a conference. She was in a beautiful gown AND comfortable — her tummy wasn't squashed in Spanx! Her best friend was helping her get dressed and said something to the effect of, "You're not going to go out there like THAT, are you?" My coach KNOWS she is ENOUGH deep inside and she said, "Yes, I am. Just like this. I'm going out there." And, she did. And proceeded to teach many other women a powerful lesson... We may not look exactly how we want to look, but we are all masterpieces and beautiful, exactly how we are. Love every inch of yourself, no matter what. *Rock What You've Got*, make the best of it and be proud. Those were my paraphrases of what I gleaned from her actions.

That coach, Liana Chaouli, in her recent book, *You are a Masterpiece: How to Dress a More Powerful and Authentic You*, teaches you to create a closet filled with tools to support your purpose, your personality, and your authenticity. She is an amazing example for women around the world. She says:

> Your wardrobe should lift you up, not beat you up. Just the thought of opening that closet door can ruin your day because the unconscious narrative will launch itself. "I'm too fat. I'm not good enough. I'm a failure." Remember you are a Masterpiece just the way you are and all of who you are is a blessed song...a song that the world needs in order to play this perfect symphony called life.

Liana encourages men and women to "make it a practice to 'see yourself', not to look at, but truly see what is there and honor your 'Be-YOU-ti-FULL' self by bringing out your own natural colors through the colors you choose to wear." She challenges readers, asking, "What are you hiding and not allowing the world to see? What are you choosing to keep small inside your spirit? What are you NOT unleashing for fear of rejection? Write it down. Speak it out, and set it free... and notice the blossoming!"

Her mission is to further and support self-acceptance, self-esteem, and self-understanding in her clients from all walks of life. She says, her goal has always been to empower people through knowledge. Liana also adds:

> I believe each human being is a Masterpiece. I believe that we are all works of genius created by the same awesome force which designed mountains and hummingbirds, the stars, and the twinkle in our eyes. And, I believe that we are constantly growing into the newest version of who we are called to be.

She encourages us to focus on our assets because it is empowering. The more your thoughts are in appreciation, the more you draw positive things to you.

A friend of mine had heard me talking about *Rock What You've Got*. One day when she was getting dressed, she was feeling bad about herself and her body when the words *Rock What You've Got* popped into her head. She told me later that when that happened, it was a quick reset to a whole new outlook that perked her up. She ended up having a great day partly because she was able to reset her perspective on herself.

In the next chapter, we're going to be talking about *Making Friends with Your Kitchen*. Keeping the components of your life working together like a well-oiled machine starts in the kitchen with your fuel and will help you seamlessly step into the Limitless Soul that you are. All of these items are a reflection, though, of knowing you are ENOUGH.

Next time you're feeling down about your body, like my friend above, remember the words *Rock What You've Got* and do a mental reset. This quick reminder will fill your soul with the message that you are enough and allow you to show up in the world honoring and radiating who you truly are. And, that's the best version of YOU. My journal entries reflect that new me as well.

Dear Body:

Thank you for hanging in there with me. I love you. I honor you. I respect you. I appreciate you and your strength. You are resilient, patient, and beautiful! You are exactly who God created you to be. I see you. I hear you. I am listening.

MAKE FRIENDS
WITH YOUR KITCHEN

*"Let food be thy medicine and
medicine be thy food."* — Hippocrates

Kitchens. Food. Love. Those words tend to go together, either consciously or subconsciously. Due to its generally central location, the kitchen has been called the heart of the home. Family members and guests gather in this space to greet one another, laugh, cry, and prepare meals that are shared in a space of love.

We pour ourselves into the food on a daily basis. Cutting, slicing, dicing food to nourish your own loved ones. As you prepare, you are unconsciously pouring your own love into the food that your family will digest. If a family isn't getting along, the kitchen can become a place of anger and unrest. Fast food meals heated up on high in the microwave become a blaring reality, mirroring their life of anger and emptiness. Although I personally love to cook healthy fresh foods, the kitchen was a source of great pain and anguish in years past. In previous journals, I even called the kitchen POISON. As you read in the *Rock What You've Got* chapter, loving my body wasn't exactly on the top of my list each day! My grandparents would weigh and measure us any chance they could while marking it on a closet door for all to see. Although meant for fun and to show the grandchildren growing, it became quite a sore spot for me, already feeling inadequate as I was.

I suspect if you're drawn to this book, you are a very busy person who may be a little confused by what your kitchen offers you. The fuel you are putting into your body may not be helping you to feel your best and to live your best life. You most likely are the person who is planning, shopping, and preparing the meals for the household as well. What you do or don't do affects not only you but others in the household and guests. In a way, you provide the fuel the rest of the family runs on.

What you eat either dumbs you down or lifts you up. It can decrease your energy, pull you into a deeper depression or encourage you to rise higher. Yes, your choice of food does all of that!

According to a National Center of Health Statistics 2003 survey, about 65.2% of American adults are overweight or obese as a result of poor nutrition. Being overweight puts people at risk for developing a host of disorders and conditions, some of them life-threatening. Poor eating (overeating, undereating, or malnutrition) can lead to a host of issues including but not limited to: high cholesterol, heart disease, diabetes, stroke, gout, cancer, compromised immune system, hair, teeth and skin problems.

Anything you can do to help facilitate healing for your body, mind, and soul should be considered. Your nutrition should be one of the first places to begin if you're feeling any of the following: depression, anxiety, low energy, extreme fatigue, dry brittle hair, diarrhea, apathy, lack of appetite, or sweets cravings.

According to the National Eating Disorders Association (NEDA):

> Eating disorders are serious, life-threatening illnesses that impact millions of people every year in the United States.
>
> Eating disorders are real, complex, and devastating conditions that can have serious consequences for health, productivity, and relationships. They are not a fad, phase or lifestyle choice. Eating disorders are serious, potentially life-threatening conditions that affect a person's emotional and physical health.
>
> People struggling with an eating disorder need to seek professional help. The earlier a person with an eating disorder seeks treatment, the greater the likelihood of physical and emotional recovery.

In the United States, twenty million women and ten million men suffer from a clinically significant eating disorder at some time in their life. By age six, girls especially start to express concerns about their own weight or shape. About 40% to 60% of elementary school girls (ages six to twelve) are concerned about their weight or about becoming too fat. This concern endures through life [Smolak, 2011].

Here are a few of the popular ways we abuse food:

Anorexia Nervosa – Inadequate food intake leading to a weight that is clearly too low.

Binge Eating Disorder – Frequent episodes of consuming very large amounts of food but without behaviors to prevent weight gain, such as self-induced vomiting.

Bulimia Nervosa – Frequent episodes of consuming very large amounts of food followed by behaviors to prevent weight gain, such as self-induced vomiting.

At one time or another I suffered from several of these eating disorders listed above, even beginning in early grade school. Nothing ever worked to heal the disorders until I began looking at the root cause, which was low self-esteem or low self-worth. For me, the kitchen represented a place of stress and disconnect.

Obviously, I had to eat but I was divided as to the best way to go about fueling my body and staying slim. Often I would not eat at all. Days would go by without any food except a cup of soup. My body would be starving and demand food, sending me into overeating to balance out the unintentional neglect. This cycle continued until my late 20s.

A few years back, I devoured the book *A Course in Weight Loss: 21 Spiritual Lessons for Surrendering Your Weight Forever* by Marianne Williamson. This book was an integral catalyst for helping me to heal the disconnect between food, my body and my soul. In it Marianne writes:

> Your true self is programmed perfectly by nature to think and behave in ways that are healthy and strong. Your job now is not only to disconnect from the matrix of addiction or compulsion, but also to reconnect with the matrix of perfection in which you were created and in which your spirit remains. This matrix of perfection is the real you. The real you is already perfect, in every aspect and in every way. You are not the problem, because you are divinely perfect.

Food was one of the very first areas where I changed my life. I've always been interested in nutrition and eating healthy but when I really committed to properly nourishing my body, I noticed an increased quality of life. Everyone has their own meaning of what healthy eating is. Mine is eating the appropriate amount of nutrition that your body needs – not too much and not too little. Enough to nourish you and fuel you for your activities.

As I began working with the steps I have outlined in this book along with Marianne's book, issues that had plagued me for decades faded away! This success has not been without much hard work — physically, emotionally and spiritually — along with working with various counselors, nutritionists, and coaches. Thankfully, I can honestly say, I am free from all descriptive eating disorders and enjoy my life, freely eating that which nourishes and heals my body.

I encourage you in this chapter to *Make Friends with Your Kitchen*. That may sound odd, but I really want you to enjoy your space and what you do there! It's important to enjoy the preparing, cooking and eating of food that nourishes you. Slow down, taste, smell, enjoy! It's a room in the house where we spend a lot of time and if it's not serving you well and making you feel awesome, then there needs to be some adjustments.

Sit in your kitchen space. How does it feel to you? Does it need to be organized? Cleaned top to bottom? Write down what it needs so that it can be a space that feels good to you. Think about what utensils you need so that you can cook your healthy meals in this sacred place.

Next, consider your own personal nutrition. Write down what you are eating for two weeks straight, then examine it closely. Make sure to include what you ate, what time, and how you felt (physically and emotionally) before and after.

Ask yourself these questions:

- Did I eat some protein first thing in the morning?
- How do I feel after lunch? Tired or energized?

- Do I get an afternoon slump and crave sweets?
- How much processed food am I eating?
- Am I eating out too much or should I consider cooking more at home?
- Am I eating when I'm truly hungry or do I eat to fill another need?
- Am I eating too many breads or other carbohydrates?

These are a few questions you should ask yourself as you examine your meal plan after a couple of weeks.

My good friend and Integrative Nutrition Coach, Laurie Runyan (HealingLuv.com), loves to reference her cooking space as *The Healing Kitchen.*

I also love how the authors at TheHealingKitchen.ca describe what *The Healing Kitchen* means to them:

> The Healing Kitchen is a place where healing begins. It's where the "Cure is in the Cupboard" and Food is used as medicine.
>
> In our family, the kitchen has always been the center of our home. It's where we play card games, discuss world issues, learn about relationship building, and prepare and enjoy good food.
>
> It's the most trafficked room in our house. We share intimate conversation, resolve conflicts, and experience

educational moments. Most importantly, it offers my family a place to come to heal and re-energize.

A kitchen that accomplishes all these things is naturally a healing place to be. It attracts people to it and creates harmony and balance to those working in it. It is inviting, peaceful and soothing and so it should be, after all, it's the place where you prepare food: food your body needs to sustain and maintain its present level of health and if necessary, heal itself.

Mostly importantly, as you are considering whether or not you should eat something, hold it, smell it, pray over it. For example, as a test, next time you are hungry, hold an apple. Ask yourself if this apple would give you energy. Feel how your body responds to that apple.

Secondly, hold a Twinkie or another processed food available in your pantry. Ask yourself if this Twinkie would give you the energy you need. See again how your body responds. Which *feels* better to you—the apple or the Twinkie? Which one would give you the nutrition and energy your body is needing? Which food item would nourish you physically?

Sometimes we get confused with seeking physical nourishment (eating) when what we really need is emotional or spiritual nourishment. Do consider that as well as you are deciding what to eat. Maybe you're not truly hungry at all, but instead need a hug!

I know this may frustrate you, but I'm not going to give you a *diet* to follow! Every BODY is different and has different needs for nourishment. As I will discuss in the chapter on Taking Charge, I've adopted a unique meal plan to facilitate healing of my thyroid, adrenals, and other hormones. I highly recommend working with an expert in the area of nutrition. You won't be disappointed!

That being said, my tried and true advice for every BODY is this:

1. If you can't pronounce it, don't eat it!
2. Consider cutting the wheat out of your diet.
3. Shop for groceries one to two times a week. As soon as you get home, prepare vegetables so they are ready to go. Cook any food items ahead for the week too.

Integrative Registered Dietitian Nutritionist and Health Coach, Carmina McGee (CarminaMcGee.com), offers some great advice to you as well:

> Our kitchens are often the hearts of our home. Just as our hearts need tending, so do our kitchens, so in turn they can become spaces that nourish us.
>
> Let your kitchen become your ally in creating a healthier you. Here are some simple strategies to help you get started:

1. Create a supportive environment by clearing out all known trigger foods that entice you into eating in a way that sabotages your health (you know what they are).

2. Stock your refrigerator and pantry with a wide variety of delicious, colorful, real foods. The kind grown on a farm, whole or minimally processed, not manufactured in a food lab. Choose fresh, organic vegetables and fruits, nuts and seeds, beans, whole grains and lean protein sources (poultry, fish, lean red meats, game meats).

3. Be kind to your bones and organs, especially your kidneys. Nix the soft drinks (yes, even diet ones), excess caffeine and sports drinks. Re-create a mini-spa atmosphere by making refreshing pitchers of filtered water infused with fresh whole berries, citrus and cucumber slices, sprigs of mint and drink to your heart's delight.

4. Always have some truly amazing dark chocolate on hand, the best you can find where you allow a square or two to slowly melt in your mouth, something in the 70% cacao range. Savor it – it takes very little to experience that little bit of bliss that is very health-giving.

So open your heart, feed your body and really start living.

As I implemented these solutions above, my mind became clearer and the mask of low self-esteem began melting away. My mood increased tremendously, depression lifted, energy increased, and an overall expanded quality of life prevailed.

Ann works full time, has four children at home and does most of the cooking for the family. Overcome with low energy and in need of assistance organizing her meals, she began making friends with her kitchen, instead of the drive-through, on her way home from work. After we talked, Ann planned ahead at the grocery store the day before, purchasing and preparing, so she knew when she walked into her house that evening that food was ready to go for dinner. Meals became a piece of cake for her and no longer a source of stress. It saved her family quite a bit of weekly money and they all began feeling quite energized because the meals were more nutrient dense.

A client, Michael, had a different challenge. Michael was struggling with afternoon sugar cravings. When we reviewed his two week food plan, it became clear he wasn't getting the proper nutrition in the morning (a balance of protein, fats, and carbs) that would set him up for a sugar-free afternoon. Michael began preparing eggs, greens, and veggies with olive oil and gluten free toast in the morning. Almost immediately he began to see his afternoon cravings dissipate, mental clarity return and his overall energy increase.

Lastly, Karen, had a history of eating disorders that kept her in fear of her own kitchen. She would hurry in and hurry out as fast as she could, preparing and eating hurriedly, so as not to feel anything while she was there. I asked her to sit in her kitchen with a notepad. Write what comes up. And, then, keep writing. Go deep. Then, go deeper. She wrote that the kitchen was the enemy, reminiscent of her childhood home full of anger and fighting. The kitchen was where most of the voices were loud. Her own kitchen didn't feel like a place of love. Instead it felt burdensome, angry, and overwhelming at times.

Subconsciously and unnoticed to her, these feelings would come up for her every time she was in her own kitchen. Until she was able to sit with it and let it come up; then she was able to acknowledge, feel the pain, and release it. This also is what I described in the Being Still chapter on feeling your feelings. Since working deeply in this area, Karen has transformed how she reacts in her kitchen and around food. She enjoys preparing and slowly eating her meals in her kitchen, which now feels like a space of love.

You too can transform your relationship to your kitchen and food! As you choose to purchase, prepare, and eat higher energy foods, you and your family will have more energy and gain mental clarity. Sugar cravings will disappear. You will begin to feel better physically and emotionally. Dry skin will disappear and you will glow! Meals will be a breeze to prepare on a moment's notice. You will save money by not eating out. And, not to mention, you will feel fabulous!

As you feel more comfortable in your own kitchen space, eating true food that nourishes your body and soul, you will naturally be drawn to surrounding yourself with a team of support and a family of love. We will be discussing this in the very next chapter. In the meantime, look at your own healing kitchen and what is produced in it as a friend, not a foe. Bless it and allow it to nourish you from the inside, out.

WHO'S IN YOUR TRIBE?

"If you want to go fast, go alone. If you want to go far, go together." – African Proverb

I'm sure, like me, when you think of the word tribe, all kinds of images come to mind. Maybe even a group of people dressed like Indians circling a large bonfire, chanting! Although the image may be a tad outdated, the purpose of a tribe in today's world still holds true. We all need a group of like-minded, supportive people around us. The first layer closest to us in our tribe should be our loved ones. We need to deliberately surround ourselves on a daily basis with these folks who support us. And, I do mean deliberately. On purpose, you need to seek love, as well as be open to receiving love when it shows up at your door.

I had a friend tell me once I was difficult to show love to. She was right. I had put up a wall around me so I supposedly couldn't get hurt again. It was easy for me to give to others but the door only opened one way. I didn't let it become a revolving door. Today, I try to be conscious so that my generous giving doesn't deplete me, and so that I am open to receiving the gifts of love others have for me.

After our loved ones, the next layers of our tribe can be other friends, mentors, and coaches you seek for support in a specific area or even health care professionals (see *Take Charge* chapter for more information on this specific team of support). When I first started working with a coach, I was always surprised when asked, "Who is supporting you? Who is helping you on a day-to-day basis?"

I was speechless. I hadn't considered that I needed someone to lean on! I was living by myself, newly divorced, an entrepreneur and an empty nester. I did feel like I was on an island by myself most days! I needed people in my life who understood me, who saw me, who knew me and my heart and what I wanted to contribute to the world and who could help me maneuver the road less taken.

Just like we hire exercise trainers, we can hire coaches for about every area of our lives including: life, business, health, nutrition, organization and time management. There are even more specific niches within each of the categories above. You name it, it's probably available somewhere! Do not ever feel like you have to go through life alone!

We are meant to collaborate, join together, and be in a tribe together. Make it a priority to find like-minded folks who you enjoy being with.

When I was a stay-at-home mom of preschoolers, it was fairly easy to find mom's groups at our local churches. However, when my youngest son entered kindergarten, I was kicked out of MOPS (Mothers of Preschoolers)! Not really, but their focus is for moms with children not in school yet. I was still needing a tribe of other moms, so I joined with a couple other ladies from our own church and started Mom2Mom. Our focus was for moms with children birth to high school age. There were many meetings where we would have 50 moms in attendance and the same number of kids!

It was great fun building a tribe of women who were like-minded and devoted to supporting one another. These women were my rock through those years of navigating the mommy roadways. I'm thrilled to report that this Mom2Mom group that began out of a love for moms and their children is still going strong decades later.

When I returned to work, my available time shrank and I struggled to fit in the right group. I was now an at-home working mom. I was alone at home but with little time to venture out and find a new group. All this was before MeetUps became popular in our area. Any extra time was spent volunteering at the kids' functions, so that provided my outlet for adult interaction. Although the volunteer groups gave me a nest to relax in, it wasn't exactly supportive on the deeper level for my day-to-day challenges that a stay-at-home mom entrepreneur encountered.

After my divorce, I gradually began building a team of support around myself. I wasn't very good at asking for help, but I had to learn to ask anyway. If they said "no," it was okay. I no longer took it personally, but I needed to at least ask. My new support group included: friends, family, doctors, nutrition experts, a finance manager, an accountant, a bookkeeper, a VA (Virtual Assistant), help keeping up with the family home (until it sold), a business mastermind group, and a book coach.

On the days that work brings my clients in virtually, I make it a point to venture out of my shell to a yoga class or to meet with friends for a walk or a cup of coffee. It's too easy for me to get all settled in for days at a time. Although I enjoy the quiet time, when I'm around like-minded people, my tribe, I am nourished on the inside.

When I look at my life now compared to even a year ago, I am surrounded by a strong tribe in layers of support that cannot be easily broken. Their love and endless support for my crazy wild life, while encouraging me to keep shooting for the moon, fills my heart. It didn't happen by accident, though. I deliberately began seeking those who would assist me and had to allow others to leave my life, as painful as that was.

If you are realizing that your *tribe* could be a little tighter or more supportive, begin to journal about what your own values and dreams are. This will help you get clarity on who your like-minded tribe folks are. Ask yourself questions like I did below:

- Who or what kind of person do I need to add into my life to help support me? Where am I lacking that someone else can help me?

- Who's on your team?
- Who supports you?
- Which loved ones surround you on a daily basis?
- Do I need a cleaning lady?
- Do I need help mowing my yard?
- Do I need someone to help me get organized?
- Do I need an exercise trainer?
- Do I need a health and nutrition coach?
- Do I need someone to check on the house while I'm away?
- Do I need to join Toastmasters to practice speaking?
- Do I need a book coach to keep me on track with writing?
- How can I connect with a friend today?
- Are there any Meet Ups in my area I could attend?
- What support in my business do I need?

What areas are you struggling in? Look at those areas and see where you could use some support. Don't be shy about reaching out.

Let down your guard to allow love and support into your heart. I realize if you've been hurt, as most of us have, then it can be scary. Sometimes we have to move through the fear into love. As I allowed myself to begin to love again, it started with ME. Not a selfish kind of LOVE, a kind of self-love that honored me, as described in the *Introduction* of this book. As I started to appreciate who I was created to be, I was better able to let others into my life who could love and support me. This group of people were folks that I deliberately set out to bring into my life. They became my team of support.

You, as well, can begin expanding your tribe (love and support) and benefit from the increased nourishment that it brings. The African proverb says, "If you want to go fast, go alone. If you want to go far, go together." Being a part of a tribe will allow you to feel loved and supported. It will also challenge you to grow into the best version of you. Take responsibility now for who you are, your values, and your beliefs and watch your tribe expand! In the next chapter, you will take those same values and apply them to taking charge of your life and your health.

In the meantime, get crystal clear on your own values and who you are. As you do that, you will naturally attract those folks who seek to do life with you.

TAKE CHARGE

*"When you take charge of your life, there is no longer
need to ask permission of other people or society at large.
When you ask permission, you give someone veto
power over your life." – Geoffrey F. Abert*

Only YOU are in charge of YOU, your health and your life. No one
else. Not your spouse, not your children, and not your doctors.
What that means is that you have to take full responsibility for your
life — physically, emotionally, and spiritually. Steve Maraboli says,
"Start walking your own walk. This journey is YOURS. Take charge
of it. Stop giving other people your power to shape your life."

You get to create the life you desire. No longer does your past have
to weigh you down.

Would you say you are running your own life? Are others walking
over your plans?

How's your health? Are you feeling listless, depressed, lethargic,
frustrated, or angry?

I totally get it. I too allowed others, even my children's schedules, to run my life for many, many years. Everyone else's demands and needs were put before my own. I own it. I completely allowed it. At the time, I didn't know I could do something different. Now, I do, and now, I do something different. You can too!

I want to encourage you today to *Take Charge* of your life and health. No one else can do this for you.

— Take Charge of Your Health —

As I've mentioned in my *Introduction*, I was quite depressed on and off over the years. Often I was listless and even unable to cry out for help. On occasions, I was even suicidal. Although I didn't want to take pharmaceuticals, it became a medical necessity. My doctor and good friend helped and guided as best she could.

One morning, I had loaded the kids into the minivan for a quick drop-off to grade school. Strangely, my new van wouldn't start. Nothing. Almost immediately frustration rose in me and my body began to have a seizure. My children watched in horror as their mom's head repeatedly hit the steering wheel and window. My body was shaking and jumping uncontrollably. Thirty minutes later, I awoke in the house vomiting. This particular seizure was caused from a reaction to an antidepressant.

As I look back at that episode, I see it was a turning point in my life. It was clear to me immediately that God and his angels were protecting us that day by not allowing the van to start. Had I ventured out on the road even thirty seconds later and then had the seizure, we probably would have ended up in the community retention pond. I am ever thankful to the Heavens for help that day. Fear for my life and my children's lives became the catalyst to get well.

I've heard it said, "The greatest wealth is health." I do believe this—wholeheartedly. Health can be described as the general condition of the body or mind with reference to soundness and vigor. Isn't that what we all seek? Thyroid/Adrenal nutrition expert, one of my nutrition mentors and a bundle of energy, Andrea Beaman, wrote in her latest book, *Health is Wealth: Make a Delicious Investment in You*, "Health is wealth literally means it's possible to have a rich life without compromising ourselves in the process. We need to learn to invest in our health on a daily basis."

Last winter, Andrea coached me through a difficult period, assisting me to heal my thyroid and adrenal issues. Although we laid a fabulous foundation for nutritional healing, I was most surprised by her focus on self-love. Her encouragement to be gentle with myself and practice self-love allowed me to *Take Charge* of my health in a loving and kind way.

Here is some *Take Charge* Advice from Andrea Beaman:

> We all have an innate healing wisdom that lives within us. I often hear it when clients sign up for health coaching.

During a session they'll say, "I know I need to eat better, I know I need daily exercise, I know I need to quit my job, I know I need to end my dead-end relationship, I know…"

Most of us know exactly what we need to do to help ourselves, but we don't take action on it.

Why not?

I believe it's because we haven't been taught to make our self and our health our number one priority, and to understand that we are responsible for our life.

Self-care is not on the agenda at our schools and it's not taught in our homes or workplace. So where the heck are we supposed to learn this valuable information?

For me, experience was the best teacher. I learned about self-care and the body's natural ability to heal through my own sickness. I was dysfunctionally programmed, like many other humans on this planet, to wait until disease came and knocked me to the floor before I made an effort to do something.

The "something" I did was not recommended by my doctors. It was considered radical and unconventional. Within fourteen days of taking responsibility for my health and incorporating self-care, I noticed improvements; clear skin, better sleep, regular bowel movements, and increased energy. Very quickly, I made the connection that within me lives an innate healing power. All I had to do was nourish it with the proper physical, emotional and spiritual food it needed to thrive.

It's been over sixteen years since making that initial commitment to self-care, and today my vibrant health (as well as the health of many clients and students) is proof that Thyroid disease, and other diseases, is curable.

The ability to heal an imbalanced or diseased condition takes patience, persistence and hard work, but you are worth it. It's time we learned how to put our health first and incorporate self-care as an option for our health-care.

Here are some simple steps to activating your body's innate healing wisdom:

STEP ONE – Take responsibility for your illness. This may sound harsh, but whatever the condition is, own it. It is yours.

STEP TWO – Become aware of your physical body and notice how it "feels" on a daily basis:

- Is it aching?
- Is your skin irritated?
- Do you have vibrant energy?
- Are you struggling to get through the day?

- Are you sleeping well?
- Is your digestive system functioning properly?

If your body is not functioning properly it's time for some serious self-care. Hire a health coach for gosh sakes!

STEP THREE – Eat clean and get off the crap! Our daily food becomes our cells, our blood, our organs, our body, and our mind. We are what we eat. And, I mean that literally! If we eat food filled with indigestible chemical substances that impair the immune system, we cannot create vibrant health. Stop spending money on healthcare that doesn't create health and put your money where your mouth is. Purchase local, seasonal food that is naturally grown and lovingly prepared. It's as simple, and as hard, as that.

STEP FOUR – After getting "clean" dig deeper into the emotional body (the chakras). It's here you can begin recognizing behavior patterns that may or may not be health-supportive. It's time to discover who you are and what is your relationship to the world around you. If I had simply changed my diet and my lifestyle, without working on my emotional body, self-healing may not have been quite as effective.

STEP FIVE – Incorporate ancient healing techniques or use any modern healing practice that works with the body/mind/spirit, and not against it. Some healing methods I use include acupuncture, massage, reflexology, aromatherapy, chiropractic, shamanic drumming, chanting, chakra healing, meditation, and many others.

Of course, there are many more steps to healing, but these are the basics. Remember, as long as you are alive and breathing you can improve any condition. When we become aware of our situation and take full responsibility for what we have created, we can flip the switch from disease – promoting to self-healing at any time.

Your body is a true masterpiece made with an intricate tapestry of hormones that run it. Our hormones are the beautiful yarn that holds the tapestry together. If one *yarn* or hormone is off balance, the others are *pulled* out of place, as well. Sometimes, we don't even realize we are experiencing declining health from unbalanced hormones until we hit a wall. This is true for men and women alike.

If you do not feel good, get help. Get help NOW! You do not have to feel this way. You do not have to be miserable the rest of your life. Although I'm not a huge proponent of taking prescription medicine, I've had to adjust my thinking in order to get well. I encourage you as well to be open-minded about your own situation.

There are times in our lives that it seems we are not strong enough emotionally to handle whatever is being thrown at us. For years, I ignored many ill-health symptoms of thyroid disease that I should've gotten help for long ago. Honestly, even though my physician (bless her) would tell me the numbers were off, I wasn't able to sustain taking care of myself. I was under immense turmoil at home and didn't want to take pharmaceuticals. I felt if I ignored the lab reports, the issue would go away.

Well, it didn't and today I'm facing even worse health issues than if I had handled things when they came up years ago. But the bottom line is, I wasn't ready. I wasn't ready to take responsibility. I was depressed and worried if I was even going to make it through the day. I really didn't care if my thyroid numbers were off. I wasn't understanding that much of it was related to how I was living my life and not loving myself.

My frustration began to overwhelm me. Frustration of being sick, yet I refused the help right in front of me. There is ALWAYS help right around you. Start with your family doctor, any doctor. Begin to get tests run that relate to your symptoms. Study, do your own research. Keep looking until you know exactly what's going on inside of you and what you need to do about it.

There is an abundance of assistance available to help you feel better if you are willing to put the work into it. You may need a quick visit to your family doctor to get things rolling or like me, you may need an entire team (physicians, specialists, nurse practitioners, acupuncturist and nutritionist) of support! Find the group that you trust and partner together with them to benefit your health. Most importantly, make sure your team is aware what each is recommending and prescribing.

Bottom line: you are in charge. This is your body and your decision what you take or don't take. If something doesn't feel right, do not dismiss this feeling. Take action to make it feel right. And, that may even mean replacing a team member or two, if necessary. There is no room for egos when it comes to your body and your health.

Your quality of life depends on it. Do not delay! You cannot expect someone else to do this work for you. Work with your team in order to make the best decisions for YOU. Every BODY is different. Ramp up your nutrition in the healing kitchen (see chapter titled *Make Friends with Your Kitchen*), get your hormone levels checked and other appropriate medical tests, meditate, exercise, and add on the appropriate supplements and medicines to assist in your healing.

Everyone knows they probably should be working out more or eating better. I challenge you to step up your workout one notch. If you're currently working out three days a week—add in a day. If you're eating a healthy breakfast, now begin eating a super nutritious lunch, one that will support you through the afternoon without sugar cravings. And, believe me, you can live a life without sugar cravings!

– Take Charge of Your Life –

We need to *Take Charge* of our health, our life, our wealth. One area affects the other. Taking charge can catapult the other areas into success or, if left to the world at large, tear them all down in one swoop.

You can feel better. You can work smarter, not longer. You can have your health and wealth.

There are many areas in which you can *Take Charge* of your life, such as:

- Your thinking, beliefs, and mindsets.
- Your *Sleep, Schedules, and Surroundings*.
- Your nutrition, health, and fitness.
- Your finances.
- Your personal boundaries.
- Your self-love and self-care.
- Your relationships in all areas of your life.

In the *Sleep, Schedules, and Surroundings* chapter, we talked in-depth on sleep, schedules and your surroundings. In the previous chapter, we focused on making friends with your kitchen and nutrition. In the chapter *Silence the Mind Chatter*, we focused on your thinking and how to silence the endless mind chatter. It's vitally important that you realize that you are in charge. Not your spouse, not your children. This is your life. You are responsible for you. You are also responsible for teaching others how to treat you.

TV personality, author, and psychologist Dr. Philip McGraw, often says, "You teach people how to treat you." Early on in my marriage I couldn't even ask my ex-husband to return a video (back in the days when we rented VHS/DVDs from movie stores). For whatever reason, I had trouble asking for help. Because of that, he never thought I needed help, so none was offered. Until I realized that:

1. I need HELP.
2. I could ask for it.
3. He could offer assistance.

Part of not asking for help is also not taking their yes or no personally. That's a whole different book! Bottom line though, I had to learn to ask for what I needed and to detach from his response.

If we aren't taking responsibility for ourselves, our actions, or our needs, then we most likely will feel like a victim. Maybe even resentful of others. Everything in our lives is connected. Our health is tied to how we take care of ourselves, which in turn affects our body and how we feel and act. One of my fabulous business coaches, Baeth Davis, reminded me recently that men have the tendency to work (business) to feel good. For women, we can't work (business) very well when we don't feel good. If we don't feel good, we're not working like we could be and our income (wealth) is decreased.

Other areas that we haven't covered in this book or chapter yet are taking charge of your finances, boundaries, and basic self-love practices.

– Finances –

People who know me well will laugh when they read that I'm writing about finances! Although I began as an accounting major in college, it didn't take long before I realized that wasn't my thing. Over the years of being married to a CPA, the daily details of bookkeeping for our family wasn't in my hands. However, since I'm on my own now, I've spent the last few years developing my own system of tracking investments, spending, and savings for myself, personally and for my business. It has been incredibly rewarding and enjoyable to be in control of the funds that God has entrusted me with.

As I look at my bank accounts, whether they are low or high, plenty or pitiful, I am thankful for the abundance. I know that with great wealth comes great responsibility—not only for myself and my family, but for the needs of the world God leads me to assist.

I encourage you as well to look at your bank balances daily. Thank God for the abundance in your checking and savings accounts. Even if it doesn't look like what you want, what you focus on will expand! Keep doing it anyway!

– Boundaries –

There were many days in the past when I allowed others to hijack my day's schedule. Obviously, this was a boundary issue for me! I wanted to keep everyone happy; peace at all costs. I believed it was what I was *supposed* to do and *had* to do. When I started delving into my subconscious beliefs that were playing out in my life, I was stunned at how much I was allowing others to control my schedule.

I would have my day packed full but would get a phone call from a friend. She needed me to watch her kids for a few hours. "Sure," I would say. Then someone else needed help with a project. Can I help with that too? "Sure," I would say. Oh wait! there's an emergency with one of the client websites. Well, not really an emergency, they only wanted to change out a picture on their website but it HAD to be done that day. "Sure," I would say. Over and over and over.

I gave myself away to please others. I gave my time, talents, money and energy to people whom I loved dearly while neglecting myself. I knew intuitively something was wrong, but I didn't know what to do about it. I just thought, this is who I am.

Examine what boundaries you have set in your life. Do you have definite boundaries placed around certain areas that are non-negotiable? And, even with those in place, we still need to be flexible for the true emergencies that pop up. Life is full of give and take moments. Even though I have a schedule, as I mentioned in

Chapter 5, I'm still very open to where and what God is leading me to do.

– Loving Yourself –

It's time for you to *Take Charge* of loving yourself. If you can't love yourself, how do you expect others to love you fully? As I mentioned in the *Introduction*, I couldn't even say the words, "self-love". Even the words made my stomach turn. I thought it utterly selfish and un-church-like to say I loved myself. I didn't believe I was *enough*. It didn't matter how many people told me I was... I couldn't believe them.

Folks who struggle with self-love can't believe they are ENOUGH. No matter how hard they try or how often they hear it from others, they can't seem to believe they are good enough. People with self-love issues may also talk a lot—usually about themselves—or seek out validation from others.

What I've learned on this journey so far though, is that self-love is instrumental in propelling you forward to the life of your dreams. It's a must to tap into your true soul's calling. Not in a selfish way, either, but rather in a way that says, "I take responsibility for who I am." If you're just beginning this self-love journey, you will benefit greatly by the practices already mentioned in this book, like being still, silencing the mind chatter, meditation, prayer, mindfulness, getting out in nature, lining up your support team, and making friends with your kitchen.

There are hundreds of ways you can begin loving on yourself. Other examples may be:

- Mirror work made famous by Louise Hay.
- Inner child work.
- Dress for success.
- Talk and listen to your body.
- Drink lots of water.
- Releasing exercises.
- Create compassion.
- Work out.
- Let go of toxins in your life.

At LimitlessSoul.com I talk about my private coaching services and VIP retreats, and how I walk you through all of the above specific areas plus more on how to love yourself more fully. We go into detail to cement self-love practices into your daily life. I want you to know that you can change.

You have the power in your mind to propel yourself forward, if you so choose. No longer do you have to let your past affect your present and certainly not your future. You can create the life and business you desire. Taking charge of your health and your life is the perfect place to begin.

When I began to *Take Charge* of my own life and health, my world took a pleasant turn I hadn't expected. My depression, energy level and health skyrocketed to a level I hadn't experienced in years.

My mind was clear and my thoughts were focused. Sleep came easily, instead of three hours a night in the past. It was effortless for me to stick to a schedule and follow through on boundaries because I knew my focus. I controlled my finances, instead of the other way around.

I felt supported for the first time because of the team around me as well as various regular self-love practices I instilled in my life. These practices allowed me to count on myself, not others, for permission to be happy.

Like myself, a client, Elizabeth, allowed others to hijack her day all too often. She committed herself to a daily workout at 9 o'clock in the morning. However, it seemed she continually got asked to attend meetings or various appointments at that time. She would forgo her commitment to herself and her health in lieu of making others happy by meeting their requests at that particular time.

I talked to Elizabeth about her self-love practice and protecting that time boundary to say she was unavailable at that particular time each day. If you are struggling with self-love, a time boundary of a workout isn't important to you, so you let other people walk all over it.

Elizabeth welcomed the opportunity for growth and began making it clear that she couldn't begin her morning meetings and errands until 10 o'clock in the morning. This was such a simple fix. However, for those of us who struggle with loving ourselves, we don't want to let others down. It's easy for us to give up commitments to ourselves because we don't think we deserve the commitment. This was a huge growth experiment for Elizabeth. With her new fixed boundary solidly in place, she occasionally had to tell others no. She felt empowered as her self-esteem increased with each exercise of this new *boundary muscle* and she quietly smiled with eagerness, loving her new self.

Depending on which areas you choose to *Take Charge* of in your life, you could expect for yourself, all or some of the following results:

- Increased energy.
- Increased health.
- Feel more positive overall.
- Increased empowerment.
- Increased self-esteem.
- Feel more loving towards yourself and others.
- Less depression.
- Less frustration.
- Less anger.
- You can feel better.
- You can work smarter, not longer.

- You can have your health and wealth.
- Feel supported.
- Clear mind.
- Focused energy and thoughts.
- Sweet, deep sleep at night.
- Feel in control of life, health, and wealth.

By assuming responsibility for your life, health, finances, boundaries, and most especially loving yourself, you have set a solid foundation. This rock solid core will assist you when life is teeter tottering. You will be able to withstand the movement to and fro explained in the next chapter, *Allowing What Is.*

Enjoy the process of taking charge of your life. No longer will you be asking others for permission to be happy! You can choose in this moment to be that joy that you seek.

ALLOWING WHAT IS

*"What if we let whatever is bothering us
to just be, not judging it as good or bad?
It just is."* – Lara Habig

When I glance back briefly over my journey of this thing called life, I can easily see a string of disappointments. Suffering. Pain. Sadness. Lost love. I also see a string of wonderful surprises and blessings interwoven to make up the tapestry of my life. Which one I choose to look at determines how I feel at any given moment.

Sometimes, all I see and feel is what is happening in this moment. If we're not careful, those unmet desires and disappointments could send us curled up in a ball, or even propel us to give up. I know, I've given up many, many times. Sometimes, several times a day!

I don't understand why disappointment has to be a part of life. Why do children get cancer? Why are there car accidents? Why do people fight and kill? I do not know, but somehow, some way, I'm determined to stop fighting these disappointments in my life and learn from them.

To be disappointed means to be discouraged by the failure of one's hopes or expectations. When you're down about a recent expectation or failed hope, life can seem awfully dismal. Hope gives you something to look forward to, to believe in, even trust. When that hope is shattered and there are pieces everywhere, the question is, what now?

That little spark of hope in me was the only thing that kept me going on most days. It seemed that was all I had. There were even numerous occasions where it felt like what small spark I had was doused. It felt like there were no embers remaining to continue. The key word here is FEEL/FELT. I have a friend who says feelings are like farts... they come and go that quickly! Something we need to remember when we are having an emotional moment.

What happens when someone lets us down? What happens when we lose our hope? Or expectations aren't met? If you are like me, you throw things around and scream for a while! Just kidding, but I bet it would feel good! As I move through difficult times, I can see a much clearer picture of my journey looking back—all of it, the pain and the pleasure. The sadness and the joy.

All of it makes up who I am today. Without one, the other can't exist. It's in the middle of the opposites that I try to reside. Centered, balanced, focused, not being attached to either/or. Just being. What if we let whatever is bothering us to just be, not judging it as good or bad? It just is. How would that feel? What would happen if we didn't react to the drama playing out around us? We allowed it to be.

By answering these simple yet complex questions as difficult moments greet us, you will bring *Your Soul's Calling* to the forefront. You will no longer be able to deny the true you. You will know who you are and why you are here on earth. You will allow what is to be. You will KNOW you are ENOUGH. No longer judging yourself or others. Instead, embracing the perfect moment as it is, no matter the emotion it produces.

It's important to:

- Recognize when we are adding to the drama of life.
- Notice what is happening around us and inside of us.
- Live in the moment.
- Recognize resistance or fear, and feel it.
- Allow what is to be and not judge it as good or bad.

Lately, I seem to be forced to answer the above questions almost on a daily basis. My roller coaster life challenges and new business have pushed me to pursue my soul's calling on a level I can hardly comprehend. This book almost didn't get written. The fear inside of me of showing the world who I truly am almost won. The resistance I was feeling to finishing this project was very close to give up mode. I've been there before. It was easy to recognize in myself.

On the morning I was finishing this chapter, a fear overtook me that I can't explain. Of course, instead of writing I was reading emails and in God's perfect timing, Dr. Christiane Northrup's email newsletter came through with words of wisdom:

> To birth something new, whether that's a baby, a book, a seminar or talk, a new relationship, or a new career, you have to have courage and faith. You also have to be ready to embrace change. Change is tough for many. As humans, we really want things to stay the same. We're creatures of habit—and so am I—even for small things. You may not be aware of this, but it's possible to give birth in an orgasmic way. Believe it or not, the energy that gets the baby in, gets the baby out. And that's true biologically, but it's also true in your personal life. To tap into this incredible and powerful energy, you'll want to learn to 'surf with' change. When you feel resistance to change, be present with it. Grieve for what's no longer going to be there. That's the only way to usher all the good stuff in. You have to feel it and move forward to give birth to the new thing. Remember that when the good stuff comes in, it brings in joy. And joy can flush out the loneliness, the fear, and the other 'stuff' that is no longer serving you. I have stood by while hundreds of women gave birth to beautiful, normal babies. Just before the time to start pushing came, nearly every woman would say, 'I can't do this! I can't do this! I don't know how to do this!' And suddenly, there was a

beautiful baby. While she didn't know how to do it with her intellect, her body and nature knew just what to do. You know how to do it, too. And your intellect may be the last thing to catch on. Have faith. Have courage. Keep breathing. And simply know that you're programmed for new beginnings.

Dr. Northrup's statement, "I can't do this! I can't do this! I don't know how to do this!" was replaying in my head over and over. That's when I combined my own advice with Dr. Northrup's encouragement, got still and began to recognize and notice what was going on. I stopped verbally beating myself up for feeling the way I did. I honored what was happening, and allowed it to just be. But then, I had to make a decision. Am I going to hide the rest of my life and deny the world my gift OR am I going to finish this book and live out my soul's calling? I chose the latter!

WHAT IS YOUR SOUL'S CALLING?

"What in your life is calling you? When all the noise is silenced, the meetings adjourned, the lists laid aside, and the wild iris blooms by itself in the dark forest, what still pulls on your soul?" – Terma Collective

Congratulations! You've made it to the end of this book! And, that my friend, is no small feat in today's busy world. You have stepped up to the challenge to investigate your limitless soul, tap into that spark inside of you, and begin to allow *Your Soul's Calling* to be revealed. You are beginning to love yourself and KNOW you are ENOUGH. What a beautiful gift you have given yourself and those in your world.

As you journey through these practices in more detail, you can dive deeper, allowing *Your Soul's Calling* to shine brighter. In your stillness, you become present in the moment, reconnecting to God inside of you. This also gives buried feelings from long ago an opportunity to surface and be healed. Acknowledging your mind chatter produces an opening to choose your beliefs and quite possibly send you on a totally new, positive life-path trajectory. Practicing consistent *Mindfulness and Meditation* will permit you to look at your life from a new perspective, providing clearer messages, increased energy, and reduced stress. Repeatedly, studies have shown that hanging out in nature can lower blood pressure, reduce anxiety, relieve stress, sharpen mental states, and even help those suffering from ADHD disorders, depression, addictions, insomnia, stress and more. It soothes, heals, restores, and even connects us. Chaos turns to organization when you implement the proper *Sleep, Schedules, and Surroundings* for your life. Daily duties enjoy a smooth flow. To *Rock What You've Got* will remind you are ENOUGH.

When you *Make Friends with Your Kitchen* and embrace a healthy relationship with nourishing your body, you will begin to see the mask of low self-esteem melt away and heal the disconnect between your mind, body and soul. Your energy will increase and an overall quality of life will begin to take hold.

As you start feeling better about who you are inside, you naturally want to be around others. Your *tribe* will challenge you to be your best YOU, while loving and supporting you. In the *Take Charge* chapter, I challenged you to assume responsibility for your life, health, finances, boundaries and self-love practices. By doing such, it will provide you with a solid core of strength as the world tilts around you. Last, but certainly not least, as you *Allow What Is*, you will step away from drama to live in the moment. Judgement, fear, and resistance will fade away when you notice the details.

As I mentioned in an earlier chapter, I couldn't say the words self-love, but I knew in my heart that I needed to implement the loving practices outlined in this book. God led me step-by-step at my own pace in order to solidify each one. The outcome has been a remarkable transformation from the inside, out. My life is finally in alignment with my soul's purpose, allowing incredible joy and happiness to embody all that I am. Self-limiting beliefs that held me back disappeared. I began to value and love myself for the first time ever. I now know I am ENOUGH. I am healthier in my mind, body and spirit. I have tools to work through resistance and fear. You too can expect the same results as you implement loving yourself practices.

You have learned you are in charge of creating your own your life. Take the pain, suffering, joy, all of it from the past, work through the practices outlined in this book, and allow your own spark or soul to speak to you. Allow *Your Soul's Calling* to reveal itself as your truest dreams come to life.

Aside from working through the steps outlined and actually getting this book finished, another dream come true for me was choosing to go on an impromptu trip out of the country for a weekend. A friend offered me free last minute tickets to a meet and greet and Def Leppard concert in Canada.

My mind chatter was telling me, "This is stupid, no one travels that far for a concert. This is silly, you have a hundred things to do so you should stay home and play it safe."

But inside I KNEW I needed to go. I love an adventure, especially when traveling is involved to a place I've never visited before with a group of new friends—that were awesome, by the way!

While watching the concert (from the third row), I realized the joy I was receiving was because the band members of Def Leppard chose to do something they LOVE. They followed their own joy and were acting on their *gift*, offering to the world their creativeness and all that they are. Not everyone in the world loves their music. However, there is a group of people who resonate with their gift and want to hear more. And, that is the way for all of us. When we are truly operating at our highest expression of who God created us to be, our soul's calling, we are offering the world our own gift. We radiate immense joy to those around us that spreads like a wildfire. Not everyone is going to understand your message, or get *Your Soul's Calling*, but those who do will feel incredible joy and bliss from your gift that you offer them.

You are ENOUGH, today, in this moment. When healed, see your past pain and suffering as the conduit to your greatest gift to the world – *Your Soul's Calling*. Don't delay in loving and valuing yourself. The world is waiting for YOU!

FREQUENTLY ASKED QUESTIONS

I lead a busy life—mother, grandmother, wife, work, and other activities. I am constantly exhausted trying to catch up with my life on the weekends but it never happens. What can I do to feel more peace and be more centered in my life?

My number one recommendation is to slow down. Cut out unnecessary activities in your life. Really look at how you are spending your time. Does it nourish you? Does it add to your life or deplete energy from you? As you begin to cut away the unnecessary activities, use that time to sit and *Be Still*. Relax on your couch. Take extra time sipping that morning coffee and watching the birds play outside the window. Focus on enjoying the moment you are in. This simple, deliberate act of Being Still became a daily ritual that I relish even today. In the stillness, I began to: be present, enjoy moments at a deeper level, feel feelings, release frustrations, reconnected to God, trust and honor myself, know that I was enough, hear God more clearly, and feel centered and energized to fulfill my soul's purpose. Without Being Still we stumble through the noise. Without Being Still we take guesses at where we should be next. Without Being Still we don't honor our self or our true calling.

I am constantly hearing lots of mind chatter. How do I know what's real? What's true? Or what to believe?

It's human nature that we all have many different voices going on in our minds, sometimes all at once! The key is deciphering what to *listen* to. I've heard it explained that our mind chatter is like a channel on a radio station. We get to choose if we want to listen to a particular station (negative, self-defeating thoughts) or change the channel to a softer, more encouraging, loving channel. My best advice with mind chatter is if it makes you feel joyful and loving then pursue those thoughts. If it makes you feel depleted, sad, depressed or angry, begin to change that channel to one that lifts you up.

What's the best way to lower my daily stress?

I recommend specific breathing techniques, *Mindfulness and Meditation* as the fastest, least expensive, and most comprehensive way to lower the stress in your life. The three techniques need to be a part of your daily life in order to help diffuse the constant battering we put ourselves through. Regardless of the route, make these part of your routine to live in peace within yourself.

I understand that being in nature is beneficial to me, but I don't have the time it takes to find nature and not sure if it's really worth the effort.

I totally understand and agree with you. What I found though, and I think you will too, is the benefits far outweigh the effort it takes to breathe fresh air and explore the natural landscapes. Spending time outdoors, whether it was resting, walking or hiking, was a reset of my body when I was feeling uneasy, stressed or unbalanced. The good news is just thinking about nature or looking at nature has pretty much the same effect as immersing yourself in it. Being outside provided many benefits for me personally and can for you as well. It helped me to mend my broken heart, release the past and old worn out patterns, and reconnect to myself and God.

I struggle with keeping to a schedule. Is it really important?

YES! Keeping a schedule that supports your life, your interests, and your family can catapult you to success beyond your wildest dreams. Daily life can be stressful enough. The best thing we can do is to honor our own personal rhythms on a regular basis as we ride the waves of life. Scheduling a good amount of sleep, work, play, relationship connection, healthy meals, and workouts every day sets you up to skyrocket your self-worth and self-love. Life is about living, loving and relationships. Schedules make certain the important people and activities in your life are a priority while the nonessentials fall away. That being said, we should be flexible with the changes the day brings while not being attached to our schedules.

My closet is a source of great pain. I run in and out of it as fast as I can. I even have beautiful clothes, but I do not wear them. I stick with black yoga pants and sweatshirts on most days. HELP!

Dressing is an act of self-love. If you're struggling in your closet and especially putting beautiful clothes on your body, you may be suffering from low self-esteem and lack of self-love. Low self-esteem shows up perfectly in how we dress (or not). If we don't feel good about ourselves, we may choose to not even show up for our life. Hence, the yoga pants as a daily uniform! Healthy self-esteem allows us to know we are enough in this moment. I encourage you to appreciate who you are, as you are. Look in the mirror when you get dressed and tell yourself, *Rock What You've Got*. Know you are ENOUGH. Right here. Right now. You don't have to be someone you are not. Be the best version of YOU. *Rock What You've Got* is about accepting and loving the body and all of who you are or have in this moment. And, when you love who you are in this moment, you naturally begin to dress to reflect that beautiful inner you and feel rockin'.

In the chapter *Making Friends with Your Kitchen*, you talk a lot about proper nutrition and how you transformed your own body by changing the food you ate. What are some of your personal favorite meals?

Glad you asked! I love to begin my day with hot lemon water with a touch of honey. Breakfast on most days are brown organic eggs and olive oil cooked with greens and other veggies. In between breakfast and lunch, I enjoy a cup of green tea or Teecino, an organic decaf coffee alternative. Lunch may be a salad with more mixed veggies, sliced avocado and grilled chicken OR a smoothie with protein powder, a cup of berries, greens, and olive oil. Dinner is usually light—grilled salmon with veggies and baked sweet potato fries OR a Chipotle-like chicken Mexican bowl that I call my "Bowl of Awesomeness", made with lime, brown rice, chicken, avocado, and whatever veggies I have in the fridge.

My snacks are normally organic gala apples, cottage cheese with cinnamon, cashews, almonds, homemade kale chips, or homemade chia seed pudding. Once a week, I splurge and make a homemade cafe latte with organic espresso, almond milk, honey and cinnamon. Because I have thyroid issues, my kale and other cruciferous veggies (broccoli, cauliflower, cabbage, brussels sprouts and collard greens) are eaten cooked, not in smoothies. I try to keep my food clean, low carb, and organic. I'm not always perfect but do my best each day. Himalayan Pink Salt and Bragg's Organic Seasoning are my spices of choice!

I am an introvert. Why do I need to be around people?

I'm asked this question often. Usually, it's in the context of, "I'm introspective and would rather be by myself than around others. Why should I reach out?" Humans by design are made to be in community. Studies have proven over and over that sick people get well not because of medicine, but because of their community and support systems. We need each other, and not only when we are sick. Even introverts benefit from being around a like-minded group of folks who can support them. If you are one who likes to be alone and focused inward, that's great. Do not change who you are! But instead, be open to the possibility of adding a few folks who have similar interests as yourself. You can begin expanding your tribe (love and support) and benefit from the increased nourishment that it brings. The African proverb says, "If you want to go fast, go alone. If you want to go far, go together." Being a part of a tribe will allow you to feel loved and supported. It will also challenge you to grow into the best version of you. Take responsibility now for who you are, your values, and beliefs and watch your tribe expand!

As a people-pleaser, I don't want to disappoint people. I want to say YES to everyone who asks me to help. HELP!

None of us want to purposely disappoint others. If you are empathic or sensitive it can be downright devastating for you to say NO to others. Honestly, though, if you do not set your boundaries, you are not doing anyone any favors. You will run yourself (health, life, family) into the ground so fast that you will be no good to anyone. Set your limits and put yourself as a priority. This is loving yourself and your family. Examine what boundaries you have set in your life. Do you have definite boundaries placed around certain areas that are non-negotiable? And, even with those in place, we still need to be flexible for the true emergencies that pop up. Life is full of give and take moments. Even though I have a set schedule, I'm still very open to where or what God is leading me to do. Please take this advice from someone who is still struggling with health issues because of saying "yes" too often. Know you are ENOUGH and you do not have to earn your way or prove you are valuable. You are enough, right here and now.

My life is not playing out at all how I thought it'd be. How do I live with disappointment and shattered dreams?

I don't understand why disappointment or shattered dreams have to be a part of life. But I do believe with all my heart that we can learn to live among the hills and valleys of life. By following the advice in this book you can overcome your challenges from a higher place of love. Next time you are feeling that disappointment or dashed dreams, begin to focus on allowing it to be in your life. Welcome it. Accept it. It's there anyway. May as well stop fighting it! Don't judge it. Let whatever is bothering you just be. This will keep you centered and balanced, not being attached to either/or. You will be able to stay constant, steady, and strong, no matter what is swirling around you. You will be able to live from a place of action, not reaction. You will reside in the eye of the storm—calm and serene.

FINAL THOUGHTS

I'm not sure if you realize I wrote this book for you. You matter to me. You knowing deep down you are ENOUGH matters to me. I pray the stories and advice in *More Than Enough: Discover Your Limitless Potential and Live Your Bravest Dream* can help you navigate your own adventures with confidence. Although this book has come to an end, you are at the beginning of your own personal journey to knowing you are ENOUGH. No longer can your past pain or suffering hold you back from your bravest dream. It can become the pathway to *Your Soul's Calling*, your life purpose. It all begins with loving yourself and knowing you are ENOUGH.

Please feel free to email me at Lara@LimitlessSoul.com anytime you feel called to reach out. I would be honored if you would share your success stories with me on how implementing the principles helped you or how I can better serve you.

Until then, always remember that you are *More Than Enough*.

136 | *More Than Enough* by Lara Habig

ABOUT THE AUTHOR

Lara Habig is on a mission to help those who don't believe they are ENOUGH realize their true value and empower them in pursuing their bravest dreams. With her books, coaching programs, workshops, VIP one-on-one weekends, and group retreats, she helps you overcome self-hatred and tap into the unlimited well of potential that exists within your Limitless Soul.

Her journey began when she found herself drowning in the river of denial and depression. Numbing herself with anti-depressants, she masked her lack of self-confidence, which only fueled more lies, anxiety, eating disorders, self-hate, and self-neglect. When her "perfect" world finally collapsed, she was forced to rebuild her life with a simple Spark of Hope.

It was that Spark of Hope that guided her to realize her soul was truly limitless and overcoming self-hatred was important. She began to believe that anything was possible. Not surprisingly, her confidence and passion for life returned with crystal clear clarity on her own divine purpose. Now, she guides others who don't believe they are ENOUGH, realize and discover their own limitless potential to live out their dreams. If you can believe in yourself with the little spark of hope that's left, you can soar into your own bravest dream. You are *More Than Enough*.

Visit www.LimitlessSoul.com to learn more about Lara Habig.

DOWNLOAD
YOUR FREE GIFT

Are you reluctant to trust yourself?

Do you struggle with anger, frustration or depression?

Is it hard for you to accept compliments?

If you said "YES!" to any of the questions above, then be sure to download your FREE BONUS GIFT -- *Loving Yourself Just For Today*, a colorful poster that you can print out and post anywhere in your home or office, or use it as wallpaper for your phone or computer.

This poster is packed with self-love practices will act as a reminder to take care of yourself in the midst of your hectic daily life. Each day as you implement one or several of the suggestions, the effects will be cumulative, allowing your confidence to soar. You will essentially begin to see yourself as worthy, valuable, and belonging in the world, deserving of happiness. And, most importantly, a belief that you are ENOUGH, as you are in this moment.

DOWNLOAD YOUR FREE BONUS GIFT TODAY:

www.LimitlessSoul.com/BookOffer

)

27128315R00100

Made in the USA
San Bernardino, CA
08 December 2015